MW00980296

The Magnificent
American West

BRIDGER WILDERNESS, WYOMING © DAVID MUENCH

BIG BEND NATIONAL PARK, TEXAS © DAVID MUENCH

FLY GEYSER, BLACK ROCK, NEVADA © LARRY ANGIER

BIG SMOKY VALLEY, NEVADA © DAVID MUENCH

Chronicles, legends & myths
Theodore Roosevelt
& Mark Twain

PUBLISHER/EDITOR: C.J. Hadley
DESIGNER/PRODUCER: JOHN BARDWELL
EDITORIAL ASSISTANT: Ann Galli
PROOFREADER: Denyse Pellettieri White

Publication of this book was made possible by generous donations from people who care about the American West to the Range Conservation Foundation, which is an educational nonprofit 501(c)(3). Excerpts and quotes from Theodore Roosevelt and Mark Twain writings are sourced from the public domain.

No part of this book may be reproduced in any form or by any electronic or mechanical means, including information storage and retrieval systems, without written permission from the publisher, except by a reviewer who may quote passages in a review.

Library of Congress
Cataloging-in-Publication Data
Hadley, C.J. & Bardwell, John
The Magnificent American West
Caroline Joy Hadley
ISBN 978-0-9647456-1-2
LCCN 2018907460
Published by Range Conservation Foundation
Carson City, Nevada.
All rights reserved.

$50 U.S.A.
Printed in China
Copyright © 2018 Range Conservation Foundation

"If you love what you do you'll never work another day in your life."
—Mark Twain

GRAND TETONS, NORTHWEST WYOMING © LARRY TURNER

EDITOR'S NOTE

Teddy Roosevelt loved hunting. He loved cowboys and ranch life. "No one, but he who has partaken thereof," he wrote, "can understand the keen delight of hunting in lonely lands. For him is the joy of the horse well ridden and the rifle well held...."

Mark Twain loved everything. He wrote: "Twenty years from now you will be more disappointed by the things you didn't do than by the ones you did. So throw off the bowlines, sail away from the safe harbor. Catch the trade winds in your sails. Explore. Dream." Twain also wrote, "Too much of anything is bad, but too much of good whiskey is barely enough."

For lovers of Roosevelt and Twain, "The Magnificant American West" will be barely enough.—*C.J. Hadley*

Contents

San Rafael River reflections, San Rafael Swell in Utah.
© David Muench

Two Voices of the West

Chronicles, legends and myths.
By Theodore Roosevelt & Mark Twain

During America's golden adolescent years between the Civil War and the Great War (now known as WWI) the nation was literally on the move, simultaneously pushing against the continental frontier and intruding on the old world.

No two men stand out more vividly in that age of expansion than Theodore Roosevelt and Mark Twain. Though they were a generation apart, came from different social and economic backgrounds and seldom met in person, they did have something in common: they went west and wrote about it.

Their experiences on the frontier would have a profound effect on each man's future, one as America's greatest storyteller and social critic and the other to lead the United States onto the international stage and into the twentieth century.

Both were prolific writers and lecturers who entertained and informed a wide audience but with very divergent styles. Twain liked to affect a rustic,

LIBRARY OF CONGRESS

Samuel Clemens, aka Mark Twain (1835-1910), at his desk back in Hartford, Connecticut in 1901. Photographer: Theo C. Marceau

homespun persona. Roosevelt was serious, eloquent and often high-minded. Twain liked a good yarn. Roosevelt liked a good moral.

Each went west for different reasons: Twain for a youthful adventure and Roosevelt to recover from personal tragedy. Both returned east with a wealth of stories but nearly empty pockets.

There were many other chroniclers of the frontier, including Bret Harte, Zane Grey and Roosevelt's friend, Owen Wister. But Twain and Roosevelt saw their western sojourns from such contrasting perspectives. Twain treated his life on the frontier as a great sport outing. Roosevelt took it all quite seriously; the ranch work and even his beloved game hunting were grave business.

Twain's words are primarily excerpted from his classic second book, "Roughing It," published in 1872. Roosevelt's accounts are taken from several books* on ranching and his shooting trips. Two very different men. Two distinct voices of the West.

—*John Bardwell*

HOUGHTON LIBRARY, HARVARD UNIVERSITY

Theodore Roosevelt (1858-1919) in Oyster Bay, New York, in 1912. He learned to genuinely love and respect average men and women "as hardy and self-reliant as any...who ever breathed." This photo by Charles Duprez was Roosevelt's favorite.

* ROOSEVELT BOOKS:
"Hunting Trips of a Ranchman" (1885);
"Ranch Life and the Hunting Trail" (1888);
"The Strenuous Life" (1899);
and "An Autobiography" (1913).

A dirt road heads toward the Humboldt Range near Oreana, Nevada.
© Larry Angier

Part I: Theodore Roosevelt

A Strenuous Life in the West

"Theodore Roosevelt Jr. was born to a wealthy and influential family in New York City in 1858. He was a sickly child, suffering from asthma and poor eyesight. Nevertheless he enjoyed a pleasant and privileged childhood, traveling to Europe and spending summers with his siblings in the country, which he much preferred to city living.

Young Teddy poses for a photo commemorating his 1881 climb of the Matterhorn.

HOUGHTON LIBRARY, HARVARD UNIVERSITY

When Teddy was about twelve, his father strongly encouraged him to build himself up with exercise and even boxing lessons. The boy took it all seriously for the rest of his life. He learned to shoot and ride, though he admitted to a lack of natural talent. But he persevered and tried to live what he later called "the strenuous life."

At Harvard he was an excellent student and a member of the boxing team. While Teddy was still at college, his father, who the boy idolized, suddenly died. Though he inherited $125,000, which could ensure a comfortable life, he refused an idle existence. He was prepared for law school but that struck him as a dull career.

Before he graduated from Harvard, he met and fell hard for Miss Alice Lee, a ravishing young socialite. They married less than a year later and set off for an ideal life. At only twenty-three, Theodore was elected to the New York Assembly where his political star continued to rise. In 1883, he and his brother embarked on a hunting trip to the Dakota Territory where he was so taken by the "Bad Lands" that he purchased a ranch and then another.

Now Alice was pregnant with their first child. In his third term in the Assembly, Roosevelt was in Albany

THEODORE ROOSEVELT COLLECTION, HARVARD COLLEGE LIBRARY

when news of the birth came, immediately followed by another telegram saying that Alice was seriously ill. At the same time, in the same house, his mother was suffering from typhus. By the time he reached home in New York City, his mother was dead and a few hours later, so was Alice. The baby, named for her mother, survived but Roosevelt was crushed. He declined to run for another term, settled his affairs, left little Alice with his older sister and headed west.

—*John Bardwell*

ABOVE: Theodore Roosevelt in the "Bad Lands," Dakota Territory, in 1885. His frontiersman outfit was tailored by Brooks Brothers and his "Bowie" knife crafted by Tiffany & Co.

BELOW, left to right: Wilmot Dow, Roosevelt and Bill Sewall in Dakota Territory in 1886.

THEODORE ROOSEVELT COLLECTION, HARVARD COLLEGE LIBRARY

In Cowboy Land

COURTESY SID RICHARDS MUSEUM, FORT WORTH, TEXAS

"**T**hough I had previously made a trip into the then Territory of Dakota, beyond the Red River, it was not until 1883 that I went to the Little Missouri, and there took hold of two cattle ranches, the Chimney Butte and the Elkhorn.

It was still the Wild West in those days, the Far West, the West of Owen Wister's stories and Frederic Remington's drawings, the West of the Indian and the buffalo-hunter, the soldier and the cow-puncher. That land of the West has gone now, "gone, gone with lost Atlantis," gone to the isle of ghosts and of strange dead memories. It was a land of vast silent spaces, of lonely rivers, and of plains where the wild game stared at the passing horseman. It was a land of scattered ranches, of herds of long-horned cattle, and of reckless riders who unmoved looked in the eyes of

"Self-Portrait on a Horse" (ca. 1890)
by Frederic Remington

© GILCREASE MUSEUM, TULSA, OKLAHOMA

"Episode of the Buffalo Hunt" (1908)
by Frederic Remington

life or of death. In that land we led a free and hardy life, with horse and with rifle. We worked under the scorching midsummer sun, when the wide plains shimmered and wavered in the heat; and we knew the freezing misery of riding night guard round the cattle in the late fall round-up. In the soft springtime the stars were glorious in our eyes each night before we fell asleep; and in the winter we rode through blinding blizzards, when the driven snow-dust burned our faces. There were monotonous days, as we guided the trail cattle or the beef herds, hour after hour, at the slowest of walks; and minutes or hours teeming with excitement as we stopped stampedes or swam the herds across rivers treacherous with quicksands or brimmed with running ice. We knew toil and hardship and hunger and thirst; and we saw men die violent deaths as they worked among the horses and cattle, or fought in evil feuds with one another; but we felt the beat of hardy life in our veins, and ours was the glory of work and the joy of living.

© GILCREASE MUSEUM, TULSA, OKLAHOMA

"Cattle Stampede on the Chisholm Trail" (1944) by Robert Ottokar Lindneux

San Luis Valley, Sangre de Cristo Range in Colorado. © David Muench

"The great grazing lands of the West lie in what is known as the arid belt, which stretches from British America on the north to Mexico on the south, through the middle of the United States. It includes New Mexico, part of Arizona, Colorado, Wyoming, Montana, and the western portion of Texas, Kansas, Nebraska, and Dakota. It must not be understood by this that more cattle are to be found here than elsewhere, for the contrary is true, it being a fact often lost sight of that the number of cattle raised on the small, thick-lying farms of the fertile Eastern States is actually many times greater than that of those scattered over the vast, barren ranches of the far West; for stock will always be most plentiful in districts where corn and other winter food can be grown. But in this arid belt, and in this arid belt only—save in a few similar tracts on the Pacific slope—stock-raising is almost the sole industry, except in the mountain districts where there is mining. The whole region is one vast stretch of grazing country, with only here and there spots of farm-land, in most places there being nothing more like agriculture than is implied in the cutting of some tons of wild hay or the planting of a garden patch for home use. This is especially true of the northern portion of the region, which comprises the basin of the Upper Missouri, and with which alone I am familiar. Here there are no fences to speak of, and all the land north of the Black Hills and the Big Horn Mountains and between the Rockies and the Dakota wheat-fields might be spoken of as one gigantic, unbroken pasture, where cow-

Late summer storm near Hell's Corner, Montana. The need for cover was almost forgotten as the power and beauty of nature approached. © Cynthia Baldauf

boys and branding-irons take the place of fences.

The road our wagons take, when the water is too high for us to come down the river bottom, stretches far ahead—two dark, straight, parallel furrows which merge into one in the distance. Quaint little horned frogs crawl slug-gishly along in the wheel tracks, and the sickle-billed curlews run over the ground or soar above and around the horsemen, uttering their mournful, never-ceasing clamor. The grassland stretches out in the sunlight like a sea, every wind bending the blades into a ripple, and flecking the prairie with shifting patches of a different green

from that around, exactly as the touch of a light squall or wind-gust will fleck the smooth surface of the ocean.

Throughout June the thickets and groves about the ranch house are loud with bird music from before dawn till long after sunrise. The thrashers have sung all the night through from among the thorn-bushes if there has been a moon, or even if there has been bright starlight; and before the first glimmer of gray the bell-like, silvery songs of the shy woodland thrushes chime in; while meadow-lark, robin, bluebird, and song sparrow, together with many rarer singers, like the grosbeak, join in swelling the chorus.

Dell'Orto cattle graze in the foothills near Jackson, California. © *Robin Dell'Orto*

The Round-Up

"During the winter-time there is ordinarily but little work done among the cattle. There is some line riding, and a continual lookout is kept for the very weak animals—usually cows and calves, who have to be driven in, fed, and housed; but most of the stock are left to shift for themselves, undisturbed. Almost every stock-growers' association forbids branding any calves before the spring round-up. If great bands of cattle wander off the range, parties may be fitted out to go out after them and bring them back; but this is only done when absolutely necessary, as when the drift of the cattle has been towards an Indian reservation or a settled granger country, for the weather is very severe, and the horses are so poor that their food must be carried along.

The bulk of the work is done during the summer, including the late spring and early fall, and consists mainly in a succession of round-ups, beginning, with us, in May and ending towards the last of October.

But a good deal may be done in the intervals by riding over one's range. Frequently, too, herding will be practiced on a large scale.

Still more important is the "trail" work; cattle, while driven from one

"The Big Country" by J.N. Swanson

range to another, or to a shipping point for beef, being said to be "on the trail." For years, the over-supply from the vast breeding ranches to the south, especially in Texas, has been driven northward in large herds, either to the shipping towns along the great railroads, or else to the fattening ranges of the North-west; it having been found, so far, that while the calf crop is larger in the South, beeves become much heavier in the North. Such cattle, for the most part, went along tolerably well-marked routes or trails, which became for the time being of great importance, flourishing—and extremely lawless—towns growing up along them; but with the growth of the railroad system, and above all with the filling-up of

"Bronk in a
Cow Camp" (1898)
by C.M. Russell

"Smoke of a .45"
(1908)
by C.M. Russell

AMON CARTER MUSEUM OF AMERICAN ART, FORT WORTH, TEXAS,
AMON G. CARTER COLLECTION, 1961.205

the northern ranges, these trails have steadily become of less and less consequence, though many herds still travel them on their way to the already crowded ranges of western Dakota and Montana, or to the Canadian regions beyond. The trail work is something by itself. The herds may be on the trail several months, averaging fifteen miles or less a day. The cowboys accompanying each have to undergo much hard toil of a peculiarly same and wearisome kind, on account of the extreme slowness with which everything must be done, as trail cattle should never be hurried. The foreman of a trail outfit must be not only a veteran cowhand but also a miracle of patience and resolution.

AMON CARTER MUSEUM OF AMERICAN ART, FORT WORTH, TEXAS, AMON G. CARTER COLLECTION, 1961.382

Round-up work is far less irksome, there being an immense amount of dash and excitement connected with it; and when once the cattle are on the range, the important work is done during the round-up. On cow ranches, or wherever there is breeding stock, the spring round-up is the great event of the season, as it is then that the bulk of the calves are branded. It usually lasts six weeks, or thereabouts; but its end by no means implies rest for the stockman. On the contrary, as soon as it is over, wagons are sent to work out-of-the-way parts of the country that have been passed over, but where cattle are supposed to have drifted; and by the

time these have come back the first beef round-up has begun, and thereafter beeves are steadily gathered and shipped, at least from among the larger herds, until cold weather sets in; and in the fall there is another round-up, to brand the late calves and see that the stock is got back on the range. As all of these round-ups are of one character, a description of the most important, taking place in the spring, will be enough.

"The stock-growers of Montana, of the western part of Dakota, and even of portions of extreme northern Wyoming—that is, of all the grazing lands lying in the basin of the Upper Missouri—have united, and formed themselves into the great Montana Stock-growers' Association. Among the countless benefits they have derived from this course, not the least has been the way in which the various round-ups work in with and supplement one another.

Our own round-up district covers the Big and Little Beaver creeks, which rise near each other, but empty into the Little Missouri nearly a hundred and fifty miles apart, and so much of the latter river as lies between their mouths.

At the appointed day all meet at the place from which the round-up is to start. Each ranch, of course, has most

Above: "The Making of a Cow Horse" © J.N. Swanson
Opposite: "The Cowboy" (1902) by Frederic Remington

work to be done in its own round-up district, but it is also necessary to have representatives in all those surrounding it. A large outfit may employ a dozen cowboys, or over, in the home district, and yet have nearly as many more representing its interest in the various ones adjoining. Smaller outfits generally club together to run a wagon and send outside representatives, or else go along with their stronger neighbors, they paying part of the expenses. A large outfit, with a herd of twenty thousand cattle or more, can, if necessary, run a round-up entirely by itself, and is able to act independently of outside help; it is therefore

at a great advantage compared with those that can take no step effectively without their neighbors' consent and assistance.

To do really effective cow-work a pony should be well broken; but many even of the old ones have vicious traits, and almost every man will have in his string one or two young horses, or broncos, hardly broken at all. Thanks to the rough methods of breaking in vogue on the plains many even of the so-called broken animals retain always certain bad habits, the most common being that of bucking. Of the sixty odd horses on my ranch all but half a dozen were broken by ourselves; and though my men are all good riders, yet a good rider is not necessarily a good horse-breaker, and indeed it was an absolute impossibility properly to break so many animals in the short time at our command—for we had to use them almost immediately after they were bought. In consequence, very many of my horses have to this day traits not likely to set a timid or a clumsy rider at his ease. One or two run away and cannot be held by even the strongest bit;

"Time to Think" by J.N. Swanson

others can hardly be bridled or saddled until they have been thrown; two or three have a tendency to fall over backward; and half of them buck more or less, some so hard that only an expert can sit them; several I never ride myself, save from dire necessity.

"**A** man on a bucking horse is always considered fair game, every squeal and jump of the bronco being hailed with cheers of delighted irony for the rider and shouts to "stay with him." The antics of a vicious bronco show infinite variety of detail, but are all modeled on one general plan. When the rope settles round his neck the fight begins, and it is only after much plunging and snorting that a twist is taken over his nose, or else a hackamore—a species of severe halter, usually made of plaited hair—slipped on his head. While being bridled he strikes viciously with his forefeet, and perhaps has to be blindfolded or thrown down; and to get the saddle on him is quite as difficult. When saddled, he may get rid of his exuberant spirits by bucking under the saddle, or may reserve all his energies for the rider. In the last case, the man keeping tight hold with his left hand of the cheek-strap, so as to prevent the horse from getting his head down until he is fairly seated, swings himself quickly into the saddle. Up rises the bronco's back into an arch; his head, the ears laid straight back, goes down between his forefeet, and, squealing savagely, he makes a succession of rapid, stiff-legged, jarring bounds. Sometimes he is a "plunging" bucker, who runs forward all the time while bucking; or he may buck steadily in one place, or "sun-fish"—that is, bring first one shoulder down almost to the ground and then the other—or else he may change ends while in the air. A first-class rider will sit throughout it all without moving from the saddle, quirting his horse all the time, though his hat may be jarred off his head and his revolver out of its sheath. After a few jumps, however, the average man grasps hold of the horn of the saddle—

the delighted onlookers meanwhile earnestly advising him not to "go to leather"—and is contented to get through the affair in any shape provided he can escape without being thrown off. An accident is of necessity borne with a broad grin, as any attempt to resent the raillery of the bystanders—which is perfectly good-humored—would be apt to result disastrously.

"In the morning the cook is preparing breakfast long before the first glimmer of dawn. As soon as it is ready, probably about three o'clock, he utters a long-drawn shout, and all the

PRIVATE COLLECTION, IMAGE COURTESY OF GERALD PETERS GALLERY, SANTA FE, NEW MEXICO

"A Slick Rider" (1905) by C.M. Russell

sleepers feel it is time to be up on the instant, for they know there can be no such thing as delay on the round-up, under penalty of being set afoot. Accordingly, they bundle out, rubbing their eyes and yawning, draw on their boots and trousers—if they have taken the latter off—roll up and cord their bedding, and usually without any attempt at washing crowd over to the little smoldering fire, which is placed in a hole dug in the ground, so that there may be no risk of its spreading. The men are rarely

A modern cowboy, working much like Roosevelt's cowboys, sorts cattle on the open plains near Cleveland, Montana. © Todd Klassy

very hungry at breakfast, and it is a meal that has to be eaten in shortest order, so it is perhaps the least important. Each man, as he comes up, grasps a tin cup and plate from the mess-box, pours out his tea or coffee, with sugar, but, of course, no milk, helps himself to one or two of the biscuits that have been

baked in a Dutch oven, and perhaps also to a slice of the fat pork swimming in the grease of the frying-pan, ladles himself out some beans, if there are any, and squats down on the ground to eat his breakfast. The meal is not an elaborate one; nevertheless a man will have to hurry if he wishes to eat it before hearing the foreman sing out, "Come, boys, catch your horses"; when he must drop everything and run out to the wagon with his lariat.

As soon as, or even before, the last circle riders have come in and have snatched a few hasty mouthfuls to serve as their midday meal, we begin to work the herd—or herds, if the one herd would be of too unwieldy size. The animals are held in a compact bunch, most of the riders forming a ring outside, while a couple from each ranch successively look the herds through and cut out those marked with their own brand. It is difficult, in such a mass of moving beasts—for they do not stay still, but keep weaving in and out among each other—to find all of one's own animals: a man must have natural gifts, as well as great experience, before he becomes a good brand-reader and is able really to "clean up a herd"—that is, be sure he has left nothing of his own in it.

To do good work in cutting out from a herd, not only should the rider be a good horseman, but he should also have a skillful, thoroughly trained horse. A good cutting pony is not common, and is generally too valuable to be used any-

© GILCREASE MUSEUM, TULSA, OKLAHOMA

"Camp Cook's Troubles"
(1912) by C.M. Russell

whistles through the air, and settles round the object with almost infallible certainty. Mexicans make the best ropers; but some Texans are very little behind them. A good horse takes as much interest in the work as does his rider, and the instant the noose settles over the victim wheels and braces himself to meet the shock, standing with his legs firmly planted, the steer or cow being thrown with a jerk. An unskillful rider and untrained horse will often themselves be thrown when the strain comes.

where but in the herd. Such as one enters thoroughly into the spirit of the thing, and finds out immediately the animal his master is after: he will then follow it closely of his own accord through every wheel and double at top speed. When looking through the herd, it is necessary to move slowly; and when any animal is found it is taken to the outskirts at a walk, so as not to alarm the others. Once at the outside, however, the cowboy has to ride like lightning; for as soon as the beast he is after finds itself separated from its companions it endeavors to break back among them, and a young, range-raised steer or heifer runs like a deer. In cutting out a cow and a calf two men have to work together. As the animals of a brand are cut out they are received and held apart by some rider detailed for the purpose, who is said to be "holding the cut."

A good roper will hurl out the coil with marvelous accuracy and force; it fairly

"Every morning certain riders are detached to drive and to guard the day herd, which is most monotonous work, the men being on from four in the morning till eight in the evening, the only rest coming at dinnertime, when they change horses.

From eight in the evening till four in the morning the day herd becomes a night herd. Each wagon in succession undertakes to guard it for a night, dividing the time into watches of two hours apiece, a couple of riders taking each watch. This is generally chilly and tedious; but at times it is accompanied by intense excitement and danger, when

Oregon buckaroos with cigarettes and cigars, ca. 1900. © Tom Robinson, HistoricPhotoArchive.net

the cattle become stampeded, whether by storm or otherwise.

Usually the watch passes off without incident, but on rare occasions the cattle become restless and prone to stampede. Anything may then start them—the plunge of a horse, the sudden approach of a coyote, or the arrival of some outside steers or cows that have smelt them and come up. Every animal in the herd will be on its feet in an instant, as if by an electric shock, and off with a rush, horns and tail up. Then, no matter how rough the ground nor how pitchy black the night, the cowboys must ride for all there is in them and spare neither their own nor their horses' necks. Perhaps their charges break away and are lost altogether; perhaps, by desperate galloping, they may head them off, get them running in a circle, and finally stop them. Once stopped, they may break again, and possibly divide up, one cowboy, perhaps, following each band. I have known six such stops and renewed stampedes to take place in one night, the cowboy staying with his ever-diminishing herd of steers until daybreak, when he managed to get them under control again, and, by careful humoring of his jaded, staggering horse, finally brought those that were left back to the camp, several miles distant. The riding in these night stampedes is wild and dangerous to a degree, especially if the man gets caught in the rush of the beasts. It also frequently necessitates an immense amount of work in collecting the scattered animals.

On one such occasion a small party of us were thirty-six hours in the saddle, dismounting only to change horses or to eat. We were almost worn out at the end of the time; but it must be kept in mind that for a long spell of such work a stock-saddle is far less tiring than the ordinary Eastern or English one, and in every way superior to it.

"But though there is much work and hardship, rough fare, monotony, and exposure connected with the round-up, yet there are few men who do not look forward to it and back to it with pleasure. The only fault to be found is that the hours of work are so long that one does not usually have enough time to sleep. The food, if rough, is good: beef, bread, pork, beans, coffee or tea, always canned tomatoes, and often rice, canned corn, or  sauce made from dried apples. The men are good-humored, bold, and thoroughly interested in their business, continually vying with one another in the effort to see which can do the work best. It is superbly health-giving, and is full of excitement and adventure, calling for the exhibition of pluck, self-reliance, hardihood, and dashing horsemanship; and of all forms of physical labor the easiest and pleasantest is to sit in the saddle.

© TERRI ARINGTON

Arizona cowpunchers catch horses out of the remuda at the O RO Ranch in Prescott. Matt Bruton is the roper. © Kathy McCraine

"I never became a good roper, nor more than an average rider, according to ranch standards. Of course a man on a ranch has to ride a good many bad horses, and is bound to encounter a certain number of accidents, and of these I had my share, at one time cracking a rib, and on another occasion the point of my shoulder. We were hundreds of miles from a doctor, and each time, as I was on the round-up, I had to get through my work for the next few weeks as best I could, until the injury healed of itself.

When I had the opportunity I broke my own horses, doing it gently and gradually and spending much time over it, and choosing the horses that seemed gentle to begin with. With these horses I never had any difficulty. But frequently there was neither time nor opportunity to handle our mounts so elaborately. We might get a band of horses, each having been bridled and saddled two or three times, but none of them having been broken beyond the extent implied in this bridling and saddling.

"A first-class hand will, unaided, rope, throw, and tie down a cow or steer in wonderfully short time; one of the favorite tests of competitive skill among the cowboys is the speed with which this feat can be accomplished. Usually, however, one man ropes the animal by the head and another at the same time gets the loop of his lariat over one or both its hind legs, when it is twisted over and stretched out in a second.

Travis Shipp drags a calf to the branding fire at Jones Tank on the O RO Ranch in Prescott, Arizona. © Kathy McCraine

Bailey Kimball stirs up a dust storm during spring branding at the Howard Mesa Cattle Company in Williams, Arizona. © Kathy McCraine

The Cowboy

"The cowboys form a class by themselves, and are now quite as typical representatives of the wilder side of Western life, as were a few years ago the skin-clad hunters and trappers. They are mostly of native birth, and although there are among them wild spirits from every land, yet the latter soon become undistinguishable from their American companions, for these plainsmen are far from being so heterogeneous a people as is commonly supposed. On the contrary, all have a certain curious similarity to each other; existence in the west seems to put the same stamp upon each and every one of them. Sinewy, hardy, self-reliant, their life forces them to be both daring and adventurous, and the passing over their heads of a few years leaves printed on their faces certain lines which tell of dangers quietly fronted and hardships uncomplainingly endured.

The cowboy's dress is both picturesque and serviceable, and, like many of the terms of his pursuit, is partly of Hispano-Mexican origin. It consists of a broad felt hat, a flannel shirt, with a bright silk handkerchief loosely knotted round the neck, trousers tucked into high-heeled boots, and a pair of leather "shaps" (chaperajos) or heavy riding overalls. Great spurs and a large-calibre revolver complete the costume. For horse gear there is a cruel curb bit, and a very strong, heavy saddle with high pommel and cantle. This saddle seems needlessly weighty, but the work is so rough as to make strength the first requisite. A small pack is usually carried behind it; also saddle pockets, or small saddle-bags; and there are leather strings where-

Jamie Wood cowboys for the 7 Up Ranch Division of Campwood Cattle Company in Prescott, Arizona.
© Kathy McCraine

Oregon buckaroo and Harney County rancher Frank Morgan in the mid-1920s.
He was born in 1905. © Tom Robinson, HistoricPhotoArchive.net

with to fasten the loops of the raw-hide lariat. The pommel has to be stout, as one end of the lariat is twisted round it when work is to be done, and the strain upon it is tremendous when a vigorous steer has been roped, or when, as is often the case, a wagon gets stuck and the team has to be helped out by one of the riders hauling from the saddle. A ranchman or foreman dresses precisely like the cowboys, except that the materials are finer, the saddle leather being handsomely carved, the spurs, bit, and revolver silver-mounted, the shaps of seal-skin, etc. The revolver was formerly a necessity, to protect the owner from Indians and other human foes; this is still the case in a few places, but, as a rule, it is now carried merely from habit, or to kill rattlesnakes, or on the chance of falling in with a wolf or coyote, while not unfrequently it is used to add game to the cowboy's not too varied bill of fare.

"A cowboy will not submit tamely to an insult, and is ever ready to avenge his own wrongs; nor has he an overwrought fear of shedding blood. He possesses, in fact, few of the emasculated, milk-and-water moralities admired by the pseudo-philanthropists; but he does possess to a very high degree, the stern, manly qualities that are invaluable to a nation."

—Theodore Roosevelt

Cow camp with the Peter French crew at the chuck wagon in Harney County, Oregon, in the late 1800s. © Tom Robinson, HistoricPhotoArchive.net

Joel Smith chops ice on the New Mexico "tundra" at the Palo Blanco Ranch in Colfax County. © *Chesna Smith*

Winter Weather

"When the days have dwindled to their shortest, and the nights seem never ending, then all the great northern plains are changed into an abode of iron desolation. Sometimes furious gales blow out of the north, driving before them the clouds of blinding snow-dust, wrapping the mantle of death round every unsheltered being that faces their unshackled anger. They roar in a thunderous bass as they sweep across the prairie or whirl through the naked cañons; they shiver the great brittle cotton-woods, and beneath their rough touch the icy limbs of the pines that cluster in the gorges sing like the chords of an Aeolian harp. Again, in the coldest midwinter weather, not a breath of wind may stir; and then the still, merciless, terrible cold that broods over the earth like the shadow of silent death seems even more dreadful in its gloomy rigor than is the lawless madness of the storms. All the land is like granite; the great rivers stand still in their beds, as if turned to frosted steel. In the long nights there is no sound to break the lifeless silence. Under the ceaseless, shifting play of the Northern Lights, or lighted only by the wintry brilliance of the stars, the snow-clad plains stretch out into dead and endless wastes of glimmering white.

Then the great fire-place of the ranch house is choked with blazing logs, and at night we have to sleep under so many blankets that the weight is fairly oppressive. Outside, the shaggy ponies huddle together in the corral, while long icicles hang from their lips, and the hoar-frost whitens the hollow backs of the cat-

"Iced Over" It's worse than cold for this cow and calf at the Palo Blanco Ranch in New Mexico. © Chesna Smith

"Curiosity has its own reason for existing." Christmas Eve and almost chow time at the Four Three Land & Cattle Company in Lusk, Wyoming. © Ashiley Lang

tle. For the ranchman the winter is occasionally a pleasant holiday, but more often an irksome period of enforced rest and gloomy foreboding.

About once every six or seven years we have a season when these storms follow one another almost without interval throughout the winter months, and then the loss among the stock is frightful. One such winter occurred in 1880-81. This was when there were very few

ranchmen in the country. The grass was so good that the old range stock escaped pretty well; but the trail herds were almost destroyed. The next severe winter was that of 1886-87, when the rush of incoming herds had overstocked the ranges, and the loss was in consequence fairly appalling, especially to the outfits that had just put on cattle.

The snow-fall was unprecedented, both for its depth and for the way it

lasted; and it was this, and not the cold, that caused the loss. About the middle of November the storms began. Day after day the snow came down, thawing and then freezing and piling itself higher and higher. By January the drifts had filled the ravines and coulées almost level. The snow lay in great masses on the plateaus and river bottoms; and this lasted until the end of February. The preceding summer we had been visited by a prolonged drought, so that the short, scanty grass was already well cropped down; the snow covered what pasturage there was to the depth of several feet, and the cattle could not get at it at all, and could hardly move round. It was all but impossible to travel on horseback—except on a few well-beaten trails. It was dangerous to attempt to penetrate the Bad Lands, whose shape had been completely altered by the great white mounds and drifts. The starving cattle died by scores of thousands before their helpless owners' eyes. The bulls, the cows who were suckling calves, or who were heavy with calf, the weak cattle that had just been driven up on the trail, and the late calves suffered most; the old range

animals did better, and the steers best of all; but the best was bad enough. Even many of the horses died. An outfit near me lost half its saddle-band, the animals having been worked so hard that they were very thin when fall came.

Montana's Big Hole Valley is said to be eleven months of winter and one month of hell. Snow started falling while shipping heifers at Dick Hirschy Cattle Company on a cool October morning, producing five inches in three hours. Evan Williams and his horse, Cantina, had a long hard day.
© Cynthia Baldauf

The Hunting Trail

"For a number of years much of my life was spent either in the wilderness or on the borders of the settled country—if, indeed, "settled" is a term that can rightly be applied to the vast, scantily peopled regions where cattle-ranching is the only regular industry. During this time I hunted much, among the mountains and on the plains, both as a pastime and to procure hides, meat, and robes for use on the ranch; and it was my good luck to kill all the various kinds of large game that can properly be considered to belong to temperate North America.

In hunting, the finding and killing of the game is after all but a part of the whole. The free, self-reliant, adventurous life, with its rugged and stalwart democracy; the wild surroundings, the

COURTESY SID RICHARDS MUSEUM, FORT WORTH, TEXAS

"Indians Hunting Buffalo" (1894) by C.M. Russell

grand beauty of the scenery, the chance to study the ways and habits of the woodland creatures—all these unite to give to the career of the wilderness hunter its peculiar charm. The chase is among the best of all national pastimes; it cultivates that vigorous manliness for the lack of which in a nation, as in an individual, the possession of no other qualities can possibly atone.

No one, but he who has partaken thereof, can understand the keen delight of hunting in lonely lands. For him is the joy of the horse well ridden and the rifle well held, for him the long days of toil and hardship, resolutely endured, and crowned at the end with triumph. In after years there shall come forever to his mind the memory of endless prairies shimmering in the bright sun; of vast and snow-clad wastes lying desolate under gray skies; of the melancholy marshes; of the rush of mighty rivers; of the breath of the evergreen forest in summer; of the crooning of ice-armored pines at the touch of the winds of winter; of cataracts roaring between hoary mountain masses; of all the innumerable sights and sounds of the wilderness; of its immensity and mystery; and of the silences that brood in its still depths.

"Thanksgiving Dinner for the Ranch"
(1888) by Frederic Remington

Pronghorn antelope, America's fastest hoofed animal, can reach speeds up to sixty miles per hour. © Alan Hart

Antelope

"Late in the season any one of us can usually get antelope in a day's hunt from the ranch by merely riding off alone, with a good hunting horse, to a great tract of broken, mound-dotted prairie some fifteen miles off, where the prong-horns are generally abundant.

On such a trip I leave the ranch house by dawn, the rifle across my saddle-bow, and some strips of smoked venison in the saddle-pockets. In the cool air the horse lopes smartly through the wooded bottoms. The meadow-larks, with black crescents on their yellow breasts, sing all day long, but the thrushes only in the morning and evening; and their melody is heard at its best on such a ride as this. By the time I get out of the last ravines and canter along the divide, the dark bluff-tops in the east have begun to redden in the sunrise, while in the flushed west the hills stand out against a rosy sky. The sun has been up some little time before the hunting-grounds are fairly reached; for the antelope stands alone in being a diurnal game animal that from this peculiarity, as well as from the nature of its haunts, can be hunted as well at midday as at any other hour. Arrived at the hunting-grounds I generally, but not always, dismount and hunt on foot, leaving the horse tethered out to graze.

The day is spent in still-hunting, a much easier task among the ridges and low hills than out on the gently rolling prairies. Antelope see much better than deer, their great bulging eyes, placed at the roots of the horns, being as strong as twin telescopes. Extreme care must be taken not to let them catch a glimpse of the intruder, for it is then hopeless to attempt approaching them. On the other hand, there is never the least difficulty about seeing them; for they are conspicuous beasts, and, unlike deer, they never hide, being careless whether they are seen or not, so long as they can keep a good lookout. They trust only to their own alert watchfulness and quick senses for safety.

In May and June the little antelope kids appear: funny little fellows odd and ungainly, but at an astonishingly early age able to run nearly as fast as their parents. They will lie very close if they think that they are unobserved. Once several of us were driving in a herd of cattle while on the round-up. The cattle, traveling in loose order, were a few paces ahead, when, happening to cast down my eyes, I saw, right among their hoofs, a little antelope kid. It was lying flat down with outstretched neck, and did not move, although some of the cattle almost stepped on it. I reined up, got off my horse, and lifted it in my arms. At first it gave two or three convulsive struggles, bleating sharply, then became perfectly passive, standing quietly by me for a minute or two when I put it down, after which it suddenly darted off like a flash.

Pronghorns follow the same migration corridors year after year, generation after generation. © Larry Turner

Moose

"The moose is the giant of all deer; and many hunters esteem it the noblest of American game. Beyond question there are few trophies more prized than the huge shovel horns of this strange dweller in the cold northland forests.

© MARK LAGRANGE/TOM STACK & ASSOCIATES

I shot my first moose after making several fruitless hunting trips with this special game in view. The season I finally succeeded it was only after having hunted two or three weeks in vain, among the Bitter Root Mountains, and the ranges lying southeast of them.

The moose is very fond of frequenting swampy woods throughout the summer, and indeed late into the fall. These swampy woods are not necessarily in the lower valleys, some being found very high among the mountains. By preference it haunts those containing lakes, where it can find the long lily-roots of which it is so fond, and where it can escape the torment of the mosquitoes and deer-flies by lying completely submerged save for its nostrils. It is a bold and good swimmer, readily crossing lakes of large size; but it is of course easily slain if discovered by canoe-men while in the water. It travels well through bogs, but not as well as the caribou; and it will not venture on ice at all if it can possibly avoid it.

Their ways of life of course vary with the nature of the country they frequent. In the towering chains of the Rockies, clad in somber and unbroken evergreen forests, their habits, in regard to winter- and summer-homes, and choice of places of seclusion for cows with young calves and bulls growing their antlers, differ from those of their kind which haunt the comparatively low, hilly, lake-studded country of Maine and Nova Scotia where the forests are of birch, beech, and maple, mixed with the pine, spruce, and hemlock.

Big Horn

"No animal seems to have been more changed by domestication than the sheep. The timid, helpless, fleecy idiot of the folds, the most foolish of all tame animals, has hardly a trait in common with his self-reliant wild relative who combines the horns of a sheep with the hide of a deer, whose home is in the rocks and the mountains, and who is so abundantly able to take care of himself. Wild sheep are as good mountaineers as wild goats, or as mountain antelopes, and are to the full as wary and intelligent.

A very short experience with the rifle-bearing portion of mankind changes the big-horn into a quarry whose successful chase taxes to the utmost the skill alike of still-hunter and of mountaineer. A solitary old ram seems to be ever on the watch. His favorite resting-place is a shelf or terrace-end high up on some cliff, from whence he can see far and wide over the country round about. The least sound—the rattle of a loose stone, a

ABOVE: One ewe keeps up with the boys. © Diane McAllister
OPPOSITE: Crowned glory. © Diane McAllister
INSET: Dufurrena Ranch ewe and lamb. © Larry Angier

cough, even a heavy footfall on hard earth—attracts his attention, making him at once clamber up on some peak to try for a glimpse of the danger. His eyes catch the slightest movement. His nose is as keen as an elk's, and gives him surer warning than any other sense; the slightest taint in the air produces immediate flight in the direction away from the danger.

Elk

"After the buffalo the elk are the first animals to disappear from the country when it is settled. This arises from their size and consequent conspicuousness, and the eagerness with which they are followed by hunters; and also because of their gregariousness and their occasional fits of stupid panic during whose continuance hunters can now and then work great slaughter in a herd. Five years ago elk

Young bulls—at about 11,200 feet on the flank of Sundance Mountain—have locked antlers and are fighting to establish dominance and gain access to cows during the mating season. © Ron Wolf/Tom Stack & Associates

were abundant in the valley of the Little Missouri, and in fall were found wandering in great bands of over a hundred individuals each. But they have now vanished completely, except that one or two may still lurk in some of the most remote and broken places, where there are deep, wooded ravines.

Formerly the elk were plentiful all over the plains, coming down into them in great bands during the fall months and traversing their entire extent. But the incoming of hunters and cattle-men has driven them off the ground as completely as the buffalo; unlike the latter, however, they are still very common in the dense woods that cover the Rocky Mountains and the other great western chains.

The gradual extermination of this, the most stately and beautiful animal of the chase to be found in America, can be looked upon only with unmixed regret by every sportsman and lover of nature. Excepting the moose, it is the largest and, without exception, it is the noblest of the deer tribe. No other species of true deer, in either the Old or the New World, comes up to it in size and in the shape, length, and weight of its mighty antlers; while the grand, proud carriage and lordly bearing of an old bull make it perhaps the most majestic-looking of all the animal creation. The open plains have already lost one of their great attractions, now that we no more see the long lines of elk trotting across them; and it will be a sad day when the lordly, antlered beasts are no longer found in the wild rocky glens and among the lonely woods of towering pines that cover the great western mountain chains.

*RIGHT: Rocky Mountain elk.
© Larry Turner*

Prairie Fowl

"The sharp-tailed prairie fowl is much the most plentiful of the feathered game to be found on the northern cattle plains, where it replaces the common prairie chicken so abundant on the prairies to the east and southeast of the range of our birds. In habits it is much like the latter, being one of the grouse which keep to the open, treeless tracts, though it is far less averse to timber than is its nearest relative, and often is found among the cottonwood trees and thick brush which fringe the streams. I have never noticed that its habits when pursued differ much from those of the common prairie chicken, though it is perhaps a little more shy, and is certainly much more apt to light on a tree like the ruffed grouse. It is, however, essentially a bird of the wilds, and it is a curious fact that it seems to retreat before civilization, continually moving westward as the wheat fields advance, while its place is taken by the common form, which seems to keep pace with the settlement of the country.

Sage grouse male strutting for a date in Lucky Boy Canyon, near Hawthorne, Nevada.
© Linda Hammond

Wolf

"The wolf is the archetype of ravin, the beast of waste and desolation. It is still found scattered thinly throughout all the wilder portions of the United States, but has everywhere retreated from the advance of civilization.

Formerly wolves were incredibly abundant in certain parts of the country, notably on the great plains, where they were known as buffalo wolves, and were regular attendants on the great herds of the bison. Every traveller and hunter of the old days knew them as among the most common sights of the plains, and they followed the hunting parties and emigrant trains for the sake of the scraps left in camp. Now, however, there is no district in which they are really abundant.

Near my own ranch the wolves have sometimes committed great depredations on cattle, but they seem to have queer freaks of slaughter. Usually they prey only upon calves and sickly animals; but in midwinter I have known one single-handed to attack and kill a well-grown steer or cow, disabling its quarry by rapid snaps at the hams or flanks. Only rarely have I known it to seize by the throat.

Five or six times on the plains or on my ranch I have had shots at wolves, always obtained by accident and always, I regret to say, missed.

Gray wolf. © Joe McDonald / Tom Stack & Associates

Big cat on the prowl. © Tom Stack / Tom Stack & Associates

Mountain Lion

"The cougar is hardly ever seen round my ranch; but toward the mountains it is very destructive both to horses and horned cattle. The ranchmen know it by the name of mountain lion; and it is the same beast that in the east is called panther or "painter."

I have never myself killed a cougar, though my brother shot one in Texas while still-hunting some deer, which the cougar itself was after. It never attacks man, and even when hard pressed and wounded turns to bay with extreme reluctance, and at the first chance again seeks safety in flight. This was certainly not the case in old times, but the nature of the animal has been so changed by constant contact with rifle-bearing hunters, that timidity toward them has become a hereditary trait deeply engrained in its nature. When the continent was first settled, and for long afterward, the cougar was quite as dangerous an antagonist as the African or Indian leopard, and would even attack men unprovoked.

LEFT: Mountain lion, aka cougar or panther. © Robert S. Michelson / Tom Stack & Associates

White Goat

"In the fall of 1886 I went far west to the Rockies and took a fortnight's hunting trip among the northern spur of the Coeur d'Alene, between the towns of Heron and Horseplains in Montana. There are many kinds of game to be found in the least known or still untrodden parts of this wooded mountain wilderness—caribou, elk, ungainly moose with great shovel horns, cougars, and bears. But I did not have time to go deeply into the heart of the forest-clad ranges, and devoted my entire energies to the chase of but one animal, the white antelope-goat, then the least known and rarest of all American game.

White goats have been known to hunters ever since Lewis and Clark crossed the continent, but they have always ranked as the very rarest and most difficult to get of all American game. This reputation they owe to the nature of their haunts, rather than to their own wariness, for they have been so little disturbed that they are less shy than either deer or sheep. They are found here and there on the highest, most inaccessible mountain peaks down even to Arizona and New Mexico; but being fitted for cold climates, they are extremely scarce everywhere south of Montana and northern Idaho, and the great majority

even of the most experienced hunters have hardly so much as heard of their existence. In Washington Territory, northern Idaho, and north-western Montana they are not uncommon, and are plentiful in parts of the mountain ranges of British America and Alaska.

*Mountain goats, aka Rocky Mountain goats, are
a subalpine to alpine species. They are sure-footed
climbers commonly seen on cliffs and ice.
© Ron Wolf/Tom Stack & Associates*

HARRY E. CHRISMAN COLLECTION

Buffalo meat and hides weren't the only useful products of the animal. Buffalo "chips" were a good source of fuel on the nearly treeless plains in Osnabrock, North Dakota in 1897.

Buffalo

"**G**one forever are the mighty herds of the lordly buffalo. A few solitary individuals and small bands are still to be found scattered here and there in the wilder parts of the plains; and though most of these will be very soon destroyed, others will for some years fight off their doom and lead a precarious existence either in remote and almost desert portions of the country near the Mexican frontier, or else in the wildest and most inaccessible fastnesses of the Rocky Mountains; but the great herds, that for the first three quarters of this century formed the distinguishing and characteristic feature of the Western plains, have vanished forever.

It is only about a hundred years ago that the white man, in his march westward, first encroached upon the lands of the buffalo, for these animals had never penetrated in any number to the Appalachian chain of mountains. Indeed, it was after the beginning of the century before the inroads of the whites upon them grew at all serious. Then, though constantly driven westward, the diminution in their territory, if sure, was at least slow, although growing progressively more rapid.

Less than a score of years ago the great herds, containing many millions of individuals, ranged over a vast expanse of country that stretched in an unbroken line from near Mexico to far

American buffalo, aka bison.
© *Therisa Stack / Tom Stack & Associates*

into British America; in fact, over almost all the plains that are now known as the cattle region.

While the slaughter of the buffalo has been in places needless and brutal, and while it is to be greatly regretted that the species is likely to become extinct, and while, moreover, from a purely selfish standpoint many, including myself, would rather see it continue to exist as the chief feature in the unchanged life of the Western wilderness; yet, on the other hand, it must be remembered that its continued existence in any numbers was absolutely incompatible with any thing but a very sparse settlement of the country; and that its destruction was the condition precedent upon the advance of white civilization in the West, and was a positive boon to the more thrifty and industrious frontiersmen.

Sparring buffalo at Yellowstone National Park in Wyoming. © Diane McAllister

Prairie Dogs

"Near where we had halted for the night camp was a large prairie-dog town. Prairie-dogs are abundant all over the cattle country; they are in shape like little woodchucks, and are the most noisy and inquisitive animals imaginable. They are never found singly, but always in towns of several hundred inhabitants; and these towns are found in all kinds of places where the country is flat and treeless. Sometimes they will be placed on the bottoms of the creeks or rivers, and again far out on the prairie or among the Bad Lands, a long distance from any water. Indeed, so dry are some of the localities in which they exist, that it is a marvel how they can live at all; yet they seem invariably plump and in good condition. They are exceedingly destructive to grass, eating away every thing round their burrows, and thus each town is always extending at the borders, while the holes in the middle are deserted; in many districts they have become a perfect bane to the cattle-men, for the incoming of

man has been the means of causing a great falling off in the ranks of their four-footed foes, and this main check to their increase being gone, they multiply at a rate that threatens to make them a serious pest in the future.

59

MULE DEER FAWNS © MARK HAYWARD

Deer

"A deer is far from being such an easy animal to see as the novice is apt to suppose. Until the middle of September he is in the red coat; after that time he is in the gray; but it is curious how each one harmonizes in tint with certain of the surroundings. A red doe lying down is, at a little distance, undistinguishable from the soil on which she is; while a buck in the gray can hardly be made out in dead timber. While feeding quietly or standing still, they rarely show the proud free port we are accustomed to associate with the idea of a buck, and look rather ordinary, humble-seeming animals, not at all conspicuous or likely to attract the hunter's attention; but once let them be frightened, and as they stand facing the danger, or bound away from it, their graceful movements and lordly bearing leave nothing to be desired. The black-tail is a still nobler-looking animal; while an antelope, on the contrary, though as light and quick on its feet as is possible for any animal not possessing wings to be, yet has an angular, goat-like look, and by no means conveys to the beholder the same idea of grace that a deer does.

Mule deer bucks in velvet.
© *Larry Turner*

Mule deer rut.
© *Larry Turner*

Grizzly Bear

"The grizzly bear undoubtedly comes in the category of dangerous game, and is, perhaps, the only animal in the United States that can be fairly so placed, unless we count the few jaguars found north of the Rio Grande. But the danger of hunting the grizzly has been greatly exaggerated, and the sport is certainly very much safer than it was at the beginning of this century. The first hunters who came into contact with this great bear were men belonging to that hardy and adventurous class of backwoodsmen which had filled the wild country between the Appalachian Mountains and the Mississippi.

But when the restless frontiersmen pressed out over the Western plains, they encountered in the grizzly a beast of far greater bulk and more savage temper than any of those found in the Eastern woods, and their small-bore rifles were utterly inadequate weapons with which to cope with him.

But the introduction of heavy breech-loading repeaters has greatly lessened the danger, even in the very few and far-off places where the grizzlies are as ferocious as formerly. For nowadays the great bears are undoubtedly much better aware of the death-dealing power of men, and, as a consequence, much less fierce, than was the case with their forefathers, who so unhesitatingly attacked the early Western travellers and explorers.

No grizzle will assail a man now unprovoked, and one will almost always rather run than fight; though if

Grizzly in Katmai National Park in southern Alaska. I was in the water as this bear pushed a wake in front of it. I was so engrossed looking through the viewfinder that I had to be warned that it was getting too close. Actually, the bear was into fishing and had no concerns about me. OPPOSITE: Grizzly in Yellowstone National Park. Both photos © Mark Hayward

he is wounded or thinks himself cornered he will attack his foes with a headlong, reckless fury that renders him one of the most dangerous of wild beasts.

"Nowhere, not even at sea, does a man feel more lonely than when riding over the far-reaching, seemingly never-ending plains; and, after a man has lived a little while on or near them, their very vastness and loneliness and their melancholy monotony have a strong fascination for him. The landscape seems always the same, and after the traveller has plodded on for miles and miles he gets to feel as if the distance was indeed boundless. As far as the eye can see there is no break; either the prairie

Theodore Roosevelt National Park in North Dakota.
© Carolyn Fox

stretches out into perfectly level flats, or else there are gently, rolling slopes, whose crests mark the divides between the drainage systems of the different creeks; and when one of these is ascended, immediately another precisely like it takes its place in the distance, and so roll succeeds roll in a succession as interminable as that of the waves of the ocean. Nowhere else does one seem so far off from all mankind; the plains stretch out in death-like and measure-less expanse, and as he journeys over them they will for many miles be lacking in all signs of life. Although he can see so far, yet all objects on the outermost verge of the horizon, even though within the ken of his vision, look unreal and strange; for there is no shade to take away from the bright glare, and at a little distance things seem to shimmer and dance in the hot rays of the sun. The ground is scorched to a dull brown, and against its monotonous expanse any objects stand out with a prominence that makes it difficult to judge of the distance at which they are. A mile off one can see, through the strange shimmering haze, the shadowy white outlines of something which looms vaguely up till it looks as large as the canvas-top of a prairie wagon; but as the horseman comes nearer it shrinks and dwindles and takes clearer form, until at last it changes into the ghastly staring skull of some mighty buffalo, long dead and gone to join the rest of his vanished race.

When the grassy prairies are left and the traveller enters a region of alkali desert and sage-brush, the look of the country becomes even more grim and forbidding. In places the alkali

forms a white frost on the ground that glances in the sunlight like the surface of a frozen lake; the dusty little sage-brush, stunted and dried up, sprawls over the parched ground, from which it can hardly extract the small amount of nourishment necessary for even its weazened life; the spiny cactus alone seems to be really in its true home.

ABOVE: Shoudi Mae Crosby moves horses to a new pasture on the X-Diamond Ranch in northern Arizona. The Little Colorado River runs through the ranch and its natural, rich grasslands in the White Mountains. Elevation of the ranch is 7,459 feet above sea level.
© *Cheryl Rogos*

From left: Blake, Bradley and Cade White at the Amador County Fair in California. They all work on their great-grandfather's spread, the Waters Ranch in Plymouth, California. © Larry Angier

"Of course what we have a right to expect of the American boy is that he shall turn out to be a good American man. Now, the chances are strong that he won't be much of a man unless he is a good deal of a boy. He must not be a coward or a weakling, a bully, a shirk, or a prig. He must work hard and play hard. He must be clean-minded and clean-lived, and able to hold his own under all circumstances and against all comers. It is only on these conditions that he will grow into the kind of American man of whom America can be really proud.

"It is the merest truism to say that the nation rests upon the individual, upon the family—upon individual manliness and womanliness, using the words in their widest and fullest meaning.

To be a good husband or good wife, a good neighbor and friend, to be hard-working and upright in business and social relations, to bring up many healthy children—to be and to do all this is to lay the foundations of good citizenship as they must be laid.

At the red barn in Copperopolis, California, after the Woosters' calf branding. From left, back row: J.W. Dell'Orto holding son Knox, Anne Dell'Orto, Pati Wooster, Steve Wooster, Tom Wooster, Kate Brooks and Justin Brooks. Front row: Waylon S. Dell'Orto, Bretta Brooks and Elsie Brooks. © Robin Dell'Orto

Natural Resources of the Nation

"**W**hile I had lived in the West I had come to realize the vital need of irrigation to the country, and I had been both amused and irritated by the attitude of Eastern men who obtained from Congress grants of National money to develop harbors and yet fought the use of the Nation's power to develop the irrigation work of the West. Major John Wesley Powell, the explorer of the Grand Canyon, and Director of the Geological Survey, was the first man who fought for irrigation, and he lived to see the Reclamation Act passed and construction actually begun.

Senator Francis C. Newlands, of Nevada, fought hard for the cause of reclamation in Congress. He attempted to get his State to act, and when that proved hopeless to get the Nation to act; and was ably assisted by Mr. G.H. Maxwell, a Californian, who had taken a deep interest in irrigation matters.

Beautiful light just after the storm has passed between Buffalo and Jackson Hole, Wyoming. © Guy de Galard

Dr. W.J. McGee was one of the leaders in all the later stages of the movement. But Gifford Pinchot is the man to whom the nation owes most for what has been accomplished as regards the preservation of the natural resources of our country.

The reclamation of arid public lands in the West was still a matter for private enterprise alone; and our magnificent river system, with its superb possibilities for public usefulness, was dealt with by the National Government not

Yellowstone trout. © Larry Angier

Island Lake in the Bridger Wilderness of Wyoming. © David Muench

*Gifford Pinchot (1865-1946) was an
American forester and politician.*

as a unit, but as a disconnected series of pork-barrel problems, whose only real interest was in their effect on the reelection or defeat of a Congressman here and there—a theory which, I regret to say, still obtains.

On June 17, 1902, the Reclamation Act was passed. It set aside the proceeds of the disposal of public lands for the purpose of reclaiming the waste areas of

*Mount Shasta and irrigated ranch fields
in Northern California.* © *Larry Turner*

OPPOSITE: *Gila Wilderness in New Mexico.*
© *David Muench*

the arid West by irrigating lands otherwise worthless, and thus creating new homes upon the land. The money so appropriated was to be repaid to the Government by the settlers, and to be used again as a revolving fund continuously available for the work.

LEFT: Winter wheat grows along County Road 11 in the rolling Dunnigan Hills northwest of Woodland in Yolo County, California. The hills are dry farmed for wheat and wine grapes and grazed by cattle.
© Larry Angier

OPPOSITE: Irrigated barley field in Rexburg, Idaho.
© Candace Cope

BELOW: Frank Busi counts cattle in the fall before moving them home from the Pardoe Allotment in Northern California's Eldorado National Forest.
© Robin Dell'Orto

Jeffrey pine reaches for Sentinel Dome in Yosemite National Park in California.
© David Muench

"When I became President, the Bureau of Forestry (since 1905 the United States Forest Service) was a small but growing organization, under Gifford Pinchot, occupied mainly with laying the foundation of American forestry by scientific study of the forests, and with the promotion of forestry on private lands. It contained all the trained foresters in the Government service, but had charge of no public timberland whatsoever. The Government forest reserves of that day were in the care of a Division in the General Land Office, under the management of clerks wholly without knowledge of forestry, few if any of whom had ever seen a foot of the timberlands for which they were responsible. Thus the reserves were neither well protected nor well used. There were no foresters among the men who had charge of the National Forests, and no Government forests in charge of the Government foresters.

The Forest Service established and enforced regulations which favored the settler as against the large stock owner; required that necessary reductions in the stock grazed on any National Forest should bear first on the big man, before the few head of the small man, upon which the living of his family depended, were reduced; and made grazing in the National Forests a help, instead of a hindrance, to permanent settlement. As a result, the small settlers and their families became, on the whole, the best friends the Forest Service has; although in places their ignorance was played on by demagogues to influence them against the policy that was primarily for their own interest.

© LARRY TURNER

"In the Grand Canyon, Arizona has a natural wonder which is in kind absolutely unparalleled throughout the rest of the world. I want to ask you to keep the great wonder of nature as it now is. I hope you will not have a building of any kind, not a summer cottage, a hut or anything else, to mar the wonderful grandeur, the sublimity, the great loneliness and beauty of the canyon. Leave it as it is."

—Theodore Roosevelt

Toroweap Overlook in Arizona.
© David Muench

"The Conservation movement was a direct outgrowth of the forest movement. It was nothing more than the application to our other natural resources of the principles which had been worked out in connection with the forests. Without the basis of public sentiment which had been built up for the protection of the forests, and without the example of public foresight in the protection of this, one of the great natural resources, the Conservation movement would have been impossible.

Great Basin National Park in Nevada.
© David Muench

Sequoia National Park in California.
© David Muench

Yosemite

"When I first visited California, it was my good fortune to see the "big trees," the Sequoias, and then to travel down into the Yosemite, with John Muir. Of course of all people in the world he was the one with whom it was best worth while thus to see the Yosemite. He told me that when Emerson came to California he tried to get him to come out and camp with him, for that was the only way in which to see at their best the majesty and charm of the Sierras. But at the time Emerson was getting old and could not go. John Muir met me with a couple of packers and two mules to carry our tent, bedding, and food for a three days' trip. The first night was clear, and we lay down in the darkening aisles of the great Sequoia grove. The majestic trunks, beautiful in color and in symmetry, rose round us like the pillars of a mightier cathedral than ever was conceived even by the fervor of the Middle Ages. Hermit thrushes sang beautifully in the evening, and again, with a burst of wonderful music, at dawn. I was interested and a little

© THEODORE ROOSEVELT COLLECTION, HARVARD COLLEGE LIBRARY

Theodore Roosevelt and John Muir in 1903 at Glacier Point in Yosemite National Park, which was first protected in 1864.

Oak tree and last light on Upper Yosemite Falls. © *Carolyn Fox*

surprised to find that, unlike John Burroughs, John Muir cared little for birds or bird songs, and knew little about them. The hermit-thrushes meant nothing to him, the trees and the flowers and the cliffs everything. The only birds he noticed or cared for were some that were very conspicuous, such as the water-ousels—always particular favorites of mine too. The second night we camped in a snowstorm, on the edge of the canyon walls, under the spreading limbs of a grove of mighty silver fir; and next day we went down into the wonderland of the valley itself. I shall always be glad that I was in the Yosemite with John Muir and in the Yellowstone with John Burroughs.

Half Dome and the Merced River in Yosemite National Park. © Carolyn Fox

"As it is with the individual, so it is with the nation: It is a base untruth to say that happy is the nation that has no history. Thrice happy is the nation that has a glorious history. Far better it is to dare mighty things, to win glorious triumphs, even though checkered by failure, than to take rank with those poor spirits who neither enjoy much nor suffer much, because they live in the gray twilight that knows not victory nor defeat.

I preach to you, then, my countrymen, that our country calls not for the life of ease but for the life of strenuous endeavor. The twentieth century looms before us big with the fate of many nations. If we stand idly by, if we seek merely swollen, slothful ease and ignoble peace, if we shrink from the hard contests where men must win at hazard of their lives and at the risk of all they hold dear, then the bolder and stronger peoples will pass us by, and will win for themselves the domination

of the world. Let us therefore boldly face the life of strife, resolute to do our duty well and manfully; resolute to uphold righteousness by deed and by word; resolute to be both honest and brave, to serve high ideals, yet to use practical methods. Above all, let us shrink from no strife, moral or physical, within or without the nation, provided we are certain that the strife is justified; for it is only through strife, through hard and dangerous endeavor, that we shall ultimately win the goal of true national greatness.

—*Theodore Roosevelt*
speech in Chicago, 1899

Mesa Verde National Park in southwest Colorado was one of the four parks designated under Roosevelt's presidency.
© Larry Turner

"In a great many—indeed, in most—localities there are wild horses to be found which although invariably of domestic descent, being either themselves runaways from some ranch or Indian outfit, or else claiming such for their sires and dams, yet are quite as wild as antelope on whose domain they have intruded."

—Theodore Roosevelt

A bunch of mustangs runs through Adobe Valley in California. © Diane McAllister

Spring wildflowers in Nevada attract a wild mare and foal. © Diane McAllister

Mustang studs fight for power and rights to the harem. © Diane McAllister

**"Always do what is right.
It will gratify half of mankind
and astound the other."**

—Mark Twain

*Mount Rainier
National Park
in Washington.
© David Muench*

Saguaro and star trails, Organ Pipe Cactus National Monument in Arizona.
© Larry Angier

"**Rattlesnakes are only too plentiful everywhere along the river bottoms, in the broken, hilly ground, and on the prairies and the great desert wastes alike.... If it can it will get out of the way and only coils up in its attitude of defence when it believes that it is actually menaced.**"

—Theodore Roosevelt

Rattlesnake ready to strike.
© *Scott Linstead / Tom Stack & Associates*

> **"Of all the things I've lost, I miss my mind the most."**
>
> —**Mark Twain**

Canyon de Chelly in New Mexico.
© *David Muench*

The Holy Ghost panel in the Great Gallery, Horseshoe Canyon, Canyonlands National Park in Utah. These pictographs date between 400 and 1100 A.D. © Larry Angier

"To one in sympathy with nature, each season, in its turn, seems the loveliest."

—Mark Twain

"Curious Horses"
Up on the bench at Mykal and Dennis Kirkpatrick's Bacon Ranch winters can be tough. Five miles from headquarters, it must seem like a long time between feedings. On this day a six-horse hitch delivered a fresh load of wild grass hay to four hundred cows and twenty-five head of horses.
© *Cynthia Baldauf*

Rising mist fills the morning air outside St. Anthony, Idaho, near the least-traveled road entering Yellowstone National Park—a dirt road that accesses its far southwest corner. This photograph was taken in late September after several days of rain. © Larry Turner

"Each season brings a world of enjoyment and interest in the watching of its unfolding, its gradual harmonious development, its culminating graces—and just as one begins to tire of it, it passes away and a radical change comes, with new witcheries and new glories in its train."

—Mark Twain

Saguaro cactus in glorious bloom in
Arizona. The largest was 78 feet tall
and well over 200 years old. The
saguaro is Arizona's state flower
and can have more than 50 arms.
© David Muench

Hedgehog cactus flowers
at Organ Pipe Cactus
National Monument in
Arizona. © Larry Angier

Red claret cup cactus flowers in Wickenburg, Arizona. © *Larry Angier*

> **"You can't depend on your eyes when your imagination is out of focus."**
>
> —Mark Twain

Mount Rainier National Park in Washington, a temperate inland rainforest, offers lots of powerful waterfalls and gorgeous fall colors. © David Muench

Olympic National Park in Washington includes high mountains with snow, glaciers and wilderness and the Hoh Rainforest, home to Roosevelt elk, black bears and other charismatic wildlife. Its coast has wild and spectacular beaches, tide pools and sea stacks. © David Muench

Branding crew at the end of the day at Frank and Colette Busi's ranch in Amador County, California. During spring calf marking and branding, more than a dozen families are there to help. From left to right: Marty Gardner DVM, Doug Joses, Gabrielle Brownlie and her son Caleb, Loree Joses, Nolan Yocum, Roger Lopez (standing on fence), John Plasse, Chanel Brownlie (blue dots), Kelsey Busi (green cap), Tash Yochheim (red cap), Andrew Crago

(dark green cap), Ben Wurm, Heather Hunt, Clinton Brownlie (hidden), Mitchel Davis, Seth Seever (sitting on hay), and Craig Joses. But wait, there's more! Frank and Colette Busi with son Ty, Colette's father, Eliott Joses, and a handful more are behind the barn about to drive pairs back into the pasture now that the work is done. © Larry Angier

Songs from red-winged blackbirds are a high slurred whistle, "Terrr-eeee." © Larry Turner

Western bluebirds can be found from sea level to high in the mountains. © Larry Turner

"**S**pring would not be spring without bird songs, any more than it would be spring without buds and flowers, and I only wish that bees protecting the songsters, the birds of the grove, the orchard, the garden and the meadow, we could also protect the birds of the seashore and of the wilderness.

—*Theodore Roosevelt*

American white pelicans are splendid fliers and can soar like eagles with their giant wings. They typically breed on islands in shallow wetlands in the interior of the continent. © Larry Turner

Great egrets are found in both freshwater and saltwater habitats. They are colonial nesters, typically placing stick nests high in trees, often on islands that are isolated from mammalian predators such as raccoons. © Larry Turner

Camping at Yellowstone "was like lying in a great solemn cathedral, far vaster and more beautiful than anything built by the hand of man."

—Theodore Roosevelt

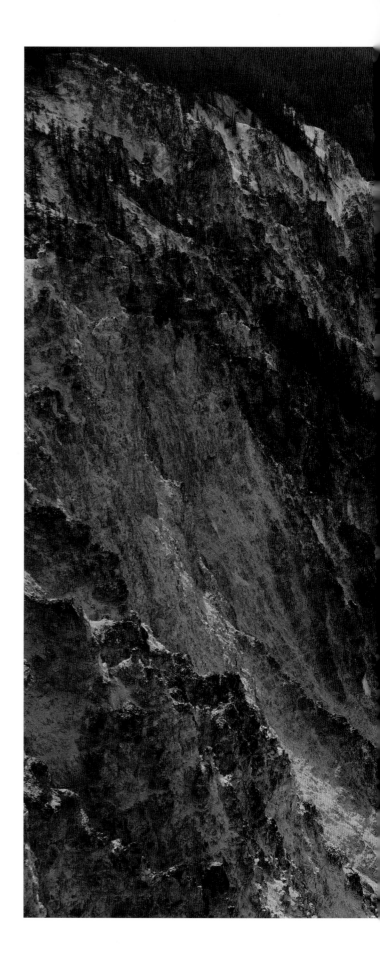

Grand Canyon of the Yellowstone in Yellowstone National Park, Wyoming.
© *David Muench*

Part II: Mark Twain

Almost a Westerner.
Almost a Southerner.

Samuel Clemens, born in 1835, grew up on the western bank of the Mississippi River, which most people considered to be the edge of the frontier. Because his home state of Missouri supported slavery, he felt some kinship with the states to the south. His family owned a slave who his father sold when their finances were stressed. As a youth, Sam didn't see anything particularly wrong with that institu-

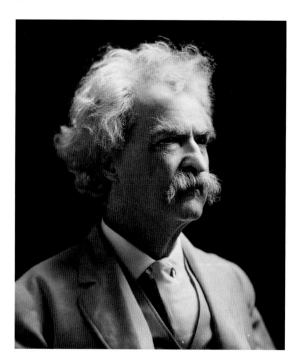

tion; it was just how things were. Later in life he bemoaned the inhumanity of slavery.

Sam's education was the basic "Three R's," the idea of higher learning was not an option. His father died when Sam was just eleven years old and his mother and siblings were looking poverty in the eye. He tried numerous jobs that a child could handle until he was apprenticed to a newspaper where he learned the skill of setting type.

When he was seventeen, the wanderlust set on him and he headed east to New York City, Washington, D.C., and Philadelphia. Eventually, having seen his fill, Sam turned back to the familiar river to fulfill an early dream of becoming a riverboat pilot, a most noble profession. He apprenticed again and eventually earned that exalted position.

Navigating the Mississippi could have been a lifelong career if the Civil War had not inconveniently come along in 1861. Civilian river traffic came to a halt and so did Sam's job. With no more work, he reluctantly joined up with a Confederate militia unit. A few weeks later he walked away from soldiering. It might be a good idea to become invisible.

While Sam was having his adventures and working the river, his older brother (by ten years), Orion, had been building a somewhat successful career in small-town newspaper publishing. He campaigned for Lincoln in 1860 and

"A Midnight Race on the Mississippi," 1860. Color lithograph by F.F. Palmer from a sketch by H.D. Manning, published by Currier & Ives (1857-1907). RIGHT: Sam Clemens, ca. 1855, when he was working as a printer in New York City. He returned to Missouri two years later and worked on riverboats. OPPOSITE: Writer Mark Twain (Samuel Clemens, 1835-1910), ca. 1900.

as a reward he was given what he considered a fine position. And he would need some help.

So begins a journey that would have Sam Clemens return as Mark Twain, author, lecturer and failed silver baron.

—*John Bardwell*

Note: In reading Twain's "Roughing It" (and anything else), be aware that the author takes some liberties and is known to play with facts. Remember what his alter ego, Huckleberry Finn, says in the opening of his adventures: "There was things which he stretched, but mainly he told the truth."

Missouri to Nevada

"My brother had just been appointed Secretary of Nevada Territory—an office of such majesty that it concentrated in itself the duties and dignities of Treasurer, Comptroller, Secretary of State, and Acting Governor in the Governor's absence. A salary of eighteen hundred dollars a year and the title of "Mr. Secretary," gave to the great position an air of wild and imposing grandeur. I was young and ignorant, and I envied my brother. I coveted his distinction and his financial splendor, but particularly and especially the long, strange journey he was going to make, and the curious new world he was going to explore. He was going to travel! I never had been away from home, and that word "travel" had a seductive charm for me. Pretty soon he would be hundreds and hundreds of miles away on the great plains and deserts, and among the mountains of the Far West, and would see buffaloes and Indians, and prairie dogs, and antelopes, and have all kinds of adventures, and may be get hanged or scalped, and have ever such a fine time, and write home and tell us all about it, and be a hero.

I dreamed all night about Indians, deserts, and silver bars, and in due time, next day, we took shipping at the St. Louis wharf on board a steamboat bound up the Missouri River.

We were six days going from St.

Louis to "St. Jo."—a trip that was so dull, and sleepy, and eventless that it has left no more impression on my memory than if its duration had been six minutes instead of that many days.

The first thing we did on that glad evening that landed us at St. Joseph

"Parting of the Ways," South Pass, Colorado. © Carolyn Fox

was to hunt up the stage-office, and pay a hundred and fifty dollars apiece for tickets per overland coach to Carson City, Nevada.

By eight o'clock everything was ready, and we were on the other side of the river. We jumped into the stage, the driver cracked his whip, and we bowled away and left "the States" behind us. It was a superb summer morning, and all the landscape was brilliant with sunshine. There was a

COYOTE © KATHY MCCRAINE

freshness and breeziness, too, and an exhilarating sense of emancipation from all sorts of cares and responsibilities, that almost made us feel that the years we had spent in the close, hot city, toiling and slaving, had been wasted and thrown away.

Along about an hour after breakfast we saw the first prairie-dog villages, the first antelope, and the first wolf. If I remember rightly, this latter was the regular cayote (pronounced ky-o-te) of the farther deserts. And if it *was*, he was not a pretty creature or respectable either, for I got well acquainted with his race afterward, and can speak with confidence. The cayote is a long, slim, sick and sorry-looking skeleton, with a gray wolf-skin stretched over it, a tolerably bushy tail that forever sags down with a despairing expression of forsakenness and misery, a furtive and evil eye, and a long, sharp face, with slightly lifted lip and exposed teeth. He has a general slinking expression all over. The cayote is a living, breathing allegory of Want. He is *always* hungry.

By and by we passed through Marysville, and over the Big Blue and Little Sandy; thence about a mile, and entered Nebraska. About a mile further on, we came to the Big Sandy—one hundred and eighty miles from St. Joseph.

As the sun was going down, we

saw the first specimen of an animal known familiarly over two thousand miles of mountain and desert—from Kansas clear to the Pacific Ocean—as the "jackass rabbit." He is well named. He is just like any other rabbit, except that he is from one third to twice as large, has longer legs in proportion to his size, and has the most preposterous ears that ever were mounted on any creature but a jackass.

When he is sitting quiet, thinking about his sins, or is absent-minded or unapprehensive of danger, his majestic ears project above him conspicuously; but the breaking of a twig will scare him nearly to death, and then he tilts his ears back gently and starts for home. All you can see, then, for the next minute, is his long gray form stretched out straight and "streaking it" through the low sage-brush, head erect, eyes right, and ears just canted a little to the rear, but showing you where the animal is, all the time, the same as if he carried a jib. Now and then he makes a marvelous spring with his long legs, high over the stunted sage-brush, and scores a leap that would make a horse envious. Presently he comes down to a long, graceful "lope," and shortly he mysteriously disappears. He has crouched behind a sage-bush, and will sit there and listen and tremble until you get within six feet of him, when he will get under way again. But one must shoot at this creature once, if he wishes to see him throw his heart into his heels, and do the best he knows how. He is frightened clear through, now, and he lays his long ears down on his back, straightens himself out like a yard-stick every spring he makes, and scatters miles behind him with an easy indifference that is enchanting.

JACKRABBIT © CAROLYN FOX

Our party made this specimen "hump himself," as the conductor said. The secretary started him with a shot from the Colt; I commenced spitting at him with my weapon; and all in the same instant the old Allen's whole broadside let go with a rattling crash, and it is not putting it too strong to say that the rabbit was frantic! He dropped his ears, set up his tail, and left for San Francisco at a speed which can only be described as a flash and a vanish! Long after he was out of sight we could hear him whiz.

Lizard Head Wilderness in Colorado. © David Muench

"Two miles beyond South Pass City we saw for the first time that mysterious marvel which all Western untraveled boys have heard of and fully believe in, but are sure to be astounded at when they see it with their own eyes, nevertheless—banks of snow in dead summer time. We were now far up toward the sky, and knew all the time that we must presently encounter lofty summits clad in the "eternal snow" which was so common place a matter of mention in books, and yet when I did see it glittering in the sun on stately domes in the distance and knew the month was August and that my coat was hanging up because it was too warm to wear it, I was full as much amazed as if I never had heard of snow in August before. Truly, "seeing is believing"—and many a man lives a long life through, thinking he believes certain universally received and well established things, and yet never suspects that if he were confronted by those things once, he would discover that he did not really believe them before, but only thought he believed them.

In a little while quite a number of peaks swung into view with long claws of glittering snow clasping them; and with here and there, in the shade, down the mountain side, a little solitary patch of snow looking no larger than a lady's pocket-handkerchief but being in reality as large as a "public square."

And now, at last we were fairly in the renowned *south pass*, and whirling gaily along high above the common world. We were perched upon the extreme summit of the great range of the Rocky Mountains, toward which we had been climbing, patiently climbing, ceaselessly climbing, for days and nights together—and about us was gathered a convention of Nature's kings that stood ten, twelve, and even thirteen thousand feet high—grand old fellows who would have to stoop to see

Mount Washington, in the twilight. We were in such an airy elevation above the creeping populations of the earth, that now and then when the obstructing crags stood out of the way it seemed that we could look around and abroad and contemplate the whole great globe, with its dissolving views of mountains, seas and continents stretching away through the mystery of the summer haze.

"We bowled along cheerily, and presently, at the very summit (though it had been all summit to us, and all equally level, for half an hour or more), we came to a spring which spent its water through two outlets and sent it in opposite directions. The conductor said that one of those streams which we were looking at, was just starting on a journey westward to the Gulf of California and the Pacific Ocean, through hundreds and even thousands of miles of desert solitudes. He said that the other was just leaving its home among the snow-peaks on a similar journey eastward—and we knew that long after we should have forgotten the simple rivulet it would still be plodding its patient way down the mountain sides, and canyon-beds, and between the banks of the Yellowstone; and by and by would join the broad Missouri and flow through unknown plains and deserts and unvisited wildernesses; and add a long and troubled pilgrimage among snags and wrecks and sandbars; and enter the Mississippi, touch the wharves of St. Louis and still drift on, traversing shoals and rocky channels, then endless chains of bottomless and ample bends, walled with unbroken forests, then mysterious byways and secret passages among woody islands, then the chained bends again, bordered with wide levels of shining sugar-cane in place of the sombre forests; then by New Orleans and still other chains of bends—and finally, after two long months of daily and nightly harassment, excitement, enjoyment, adventure, and awful peril of parched throats, pumps and evaporation, pass the Gulf and enter into its rest upon the bosom of the tropic sea, never to look upon its snow-peaks again or regret them.

We had been climbing up the long shoulders of the Rocky Mountains for many tedious hours—we started down

© CAROLYN FOX

© DAVID MUENCH

At the Continental Divide (opposite page), waters on one side flow west and east on the other. What Twain witnessed at the bifurcated spring was the Colorado River (above, in the Grand Canyon) beginning its winding trip west and south and the Arkansas River draining east to meet the Missouri, thus joining the Mississippi.

them, now. And we went spinning away at a round rate too.

We left the snowy Wind River Mountains and Uinta Mountains behind, and sped away, always through splendid scenery but occasionally through long ranks of white skeletons of mules and oxen—monuments of the huge emigration of other days—and here and there were up-ended boards or small piles of stones which

RAVEN © MARK HAYWARD

the driver said marked the resting-place of more precious remains.

It was the loneliest land for a grave! A land given over to the cayote and the raven—which is but another name for desolation and utter solitude.

At four in the afternoon we arrived on the summit of Big Mountain, fifteen miles from Salt Lake City, when all the world was glorified with the setting sun, and the most stupendous panorama of mountain peaks yet encountered burst on our sight. We looked out upon this sublime spectacle from under the arch of a brilliant rainbow! Even the overland stage-driver stopped his horses and gazed!

*The Great Salt Lake is the largest saltwater lake in the Western Hemisphere
and the eighth largest terminal lake in the world at 1,699 square miles.
The surface elevation is 4,206 feet above sea level.* © *David Muench*

"And it was comfort in those succeeding days to sit up and contemplate the majestic panorama of mountains and valleys spread out below us and eat ham and hard boiled eggs while our spiritual natures revelled alternately in rainbows, thunderstorms, and peerless sunsets. Nothing helps scenery like ham and eggs. Ham and eggs, and after these a pipe—an old, rank, delicious pipe—ham and eggs and scenery, a "down grade," a flying coach, a fragrant pipe and a contented heart—these make happiness. It is what all the ages have struggled for.

On the seventeenth day we passed the highest mountain peaks we had yet seen, and although the day was very warm the night that followed upon its heels was wintry cold and blankets were next to useless.

On the eighteenth day we encountered the eastward-bound telegraph-constructors at Reese River station and sent a message to his Excellency Governor Nye at Carson City (distant one hundred and fifty-six miles).

On the nineteenth day we crossed the Great American Desert—forty memorable miles of bottomless sand, into which the coach wheels sunk from six inches to a foot. We worked our passage most of the way across. That is to say, we got out and walked. It was a dreary pull and a long and thirsty one, for we had no water. From one extremity of this desert to the other, the road was white with the bones of oxen and

"Put your slicker on—we're gonna get wet." The day turns black as night and obstructs the view of the Bitterroot Mountains. Rain pours from the sky by the bucket and fifteen minutes later it is as if it hasn't happened at the Daniels Ranch in Wisdom, Montana. © Cynthia Baldauf

Big Smoky Valley in Nevada is about one hundred miles long and named for a haze that frequently settles there. Annual precipitation is ten inches. It is home to 2,500 people with jobs in agriculture, mining and ranching. © David Muench

horses. It would hardly be an exaggeration to say that we could have walked the forty miles and set our feet on a bone at every step! The desert was one prodigious graveyard. And the log-chains, wagon tyres, and rotting wrecks of vehicles were almost as thick as the bones. I think we saw log-chains enough rusting there in the desert, to reach across any State in the Union. Do not these relics suggest something of an idea of the fearful suffering and privation the early emigrants to California endured?

SAGEBRUSH © C.J. HADLEY

"I do not remember where we first came across "sage-brush," but as I have been speaking of it I may as well describe it.

This is easily done, for if the reader can imagine a gnarled and venerable live-oak-tree reduced to a little shrub two feet-high, with its rough bark, its foliage, its twisted boughs, all complete, he can picture the "sage-brush" exactly. Often, on lazy afternoons in the mountains, I have lain on the ground with my face under a sage-bush, and entertained myself with fancying that the gnats among its foliage were liliputian birds, and that the ants marching and countermarching about its base were liliputian flocks and herds, and myself some vast loafer from Brobdignag waiting to catch a little citizen and eat him.

It is an imposing monarch of the forest in exquisite miniature, is the "sage-brush." Its foliage is a grayish green, and gives that tint to desert and mountain. It smells like our domestic sage, and "sage-tea" made from it tastes like the sage-tea which all boys are so well acquainted with. The sage-brush is a singularly hardy plant, and grows right in the midst of deep sand, and among barren rocks, where nothing else in the vegetable world would try to grow, except "bunch-grass."

Sage-brush is very fair fuel, but as a vegetable it is a distinguished failure. Nothing can abide the taste of it but the jackass and his illegitimate child the mule. But their testimony to nutritiousness is worth nothing, for they will eat pine knots, or anthracite coal, or brass filings, or lead pipe, or old bottles, or anything that comes handy, and then go off looking as grateful as if they had had oysters for dinner. Mules and donkeys and camels have appetites that anything will relieve temporarily, but nothing satisfy.

BURRO FAMILY © DIANE MCALLISTER

"Concerning the difference between man and the jackass: some observers hold that there isn't any. But this wrongs the jackass."

—Mark Twain

Lake Tahoe

"We had heard a world of talk about the marvelous beauty of Lake Tahoe, and finally curiosity drove us thither to see it. Three or four members of the Brigade had been there and located some timber-lands on its shores and stored up a quantity of provisions in their camp. We strapped a couple of blankets on our shoulders and took an axe apiece and started—for we intended to take up a wood ranch or so ourselves and become wealthy. We were on foot. The reader will find it advantageous to go horse-back. We were told that the distance was eleven miles. We tramped a long time on level ground, and then toiled laboriously up a mountain about a thousand miles high and looked over. No lake there. We descended on the other side, crossed the valley and toiled up another mountain three or four thousand miles high, apparently, and looked over again. No lake yet. We sat down tired and perspiring, and hired a couple of Chinamen to curse those people who had beguiled us. Thus refreshed, we presently resumed the march with renewed vigor and determination. We plodded on, two or three hours longer, and at last the Lake burst upon us—a noble sheet of blue water lifted six thousand three hundred feet above the level of the sea, and walled in by a rim of snow-clad mountain peaks that towered aloft full three thousand feet higher still! It was a vast oval, and one would have to use up eighty or a hundred good miles in traveling around it. As it lay there with the shadows of the mountains brilliantly photographed upon its still surface I thought it must surely be the fairest picture the whole earth affords.

It is always very cold on that lake shore in the night, but we had plenty of blankets and were warm enough. We never moved a muscle all night, but waked at early dawn in the original positions, and got up at once, thoroughly refreshed, free from soreness, and brim full of friskiness. There is no end of wholesome medicine in such an experience. That morning we could have whipped ten such people

© DAVID MUENCH

© DAVID MUENCH

ABOVE: Emerald Bay, on Tahoe's west shore in California, is the most distinctive feature on the lake. Twain probably never saw it because he certainly would have mentioned this sight.
OPPOSITE: Sand Harbor, on the Nevada side of Tahoe, is likely the area where Twain camped, though several tourism boosters make opposing claims.

© DAVID MUENCH

as we were the day before—sick ones at any rate. But the world is slow, and people will go to "water cures" and "movement cures" and to foreign lands for health. Three months of camp life on Lake Tahoe would restore an Egyptian mummy to his pristine vigor, and give him an appetite like an alligator. I do not mean the oldest and driest mummies, of course, but the fresher ones. The air up there in the clouds is very pure and fine, bracing and delicious. And why shouldn't it be?—it is the same the angels breathe. I think that hardly any amount of fatigue can be gathered together that a man cannot sleep off in one night on the sand by its side. Not under a roof, but under the sky; it seldom or never rains there in the summer-time.

"The shore all along was indented with deep, curved bays and coves, bordered by narrow sand-beaches; and where the sand ended, the steep mountain-sides rose right up aloft into space—rose up like a vast wall a little out of the perpendicular, and thickly wooded with tall pines.

So singularly clear was the water, that where it was only twenty or thirty feet deep the bottom was so perfectly distinct that the boat seemed floating in the air! Yes, where it was even eighty feet deep. Every little pebble was distinct, every speckled trout, every hand's-breadth of sand. Often, as we lay on our faces, a granite boulder, as large as a village church, would start out of the bottom apparently, and seem climbing up rapidly to the surface, till presently it threatened to touch our faces, and we could not resist the impulse to seize an oar and avert the danger. But the boat would float on, and the boulder descend again, and then we could see that when we had been exactly above it, it must still have been twenty or thirty feet below the surface. Down through the transparency of these great depths, the water was not merely transparent, but dazzlingly, brilliantly so. All objects seen through it had a bright, strong vividness, not only of outline, but of every minute detail, which they would not have had when seen simply through the same depth of atmosphere. So empty and airy did all spaces seem below us, and so strong was the sense of floating high aloft in mid-nothingness, that we called these boat-excursions "balloon-voyages."

© DAVID MUENCH

ABOVE: Rounded boulders punctuate the shoreline, remnants left by the glaciers that gouged out the lake basin. OPPOSITE: View from the road to 10,778-foot Mount Rose.

The Washoe Zephyr

"We were approaching the end of our long journey. It was the morning of the twentieth day. At noon we would reach Carson City, the capital of Nevada Territory. We were not glad, but sorry. It had been a fine pleasure trip; we had fed fat on wonders every day; we were now well accustomed to stage life, and very fond of it; so the idea of coming to a stand-still and settling down to a humdrum existence in a village was not agreeable, but on the contrary depressing.

Visibly our new home was a desert, walled in by barren, snow-clad mountains. There was not a tree in sight. There was no vegetation but the endless sage-brush and greasewood. All nature was gray with it. We were plowing through great deeps of powdery alkali dust that rose in thick clouds and floated across the plain like smoke from a burning house.

It was two o'clock, now, and according to custom the daily "Washoe Zephyr" set in; a soaring dust-drift about the size of the United States set up edge-wise came with it, and the capital of Nevada Territory disappeared from view. Still, there were sights to be seen which were not wholly uninteresting to newcomers; for the vast dust-cloud was thickly freckled with things strange to the upper air—things living and dead, that flitted hither and thither, going and coming, appearing and disappearing among the rolling billows of dust—hats, chickens and parasols sailing in the remote heavens; blankets, tin signs, sage-brush and shingles a shade lower; door-mats and buffalo robes lower still; shovels and coal-scuttles on the next grade; glass doors, cats and little children on the next; disrupted lumber yards, light buggies and wheel-barrows on the next; and down only thirty or forty feet above ground was a scurrying storm of emigrating roofs and vacant lots.

It was something to see that much. I could have seen more, if I could have kept the dust out of my eyes.

But seriously a Washoe wind is by no means a trifling matter. It blows flimsy houses down, lifts shingle roofs occasionally, rolls up tin ones like sheet music, now and then blows a stage coach over and spills the passengers; and tradition says the reason there are so many bald people there, is, that the wind blows the hair off their heads while they are looking skyward after their hats.

Nevada dust devil. © Doug Keister

© DAVID MUENCH

Mono Lake

"**M**ono Lake lies in a lifeless, treeless, hideous desert, eight thousand feet above the level of the sea, and is guarded by mountains two thousand feet higher, whose summits are always clothed in clouds. This solemn, silent, sail-less sea—this lonely tenant of the loneliest spot on earth—is little graced with the picturesque. It is an unpretending expanse of grayish water, about a hundred miles in circumference, with two islands in its centre, mere upheavals of rent and scorched and blistered lava, snowed over with gray banks and drifts of pumice-stone and ashes, the winding sheet of the dead volcano, whose vast crater the lake has seized upon and occupied. The lake is two hundred feet deep, and its sluggish waters are so strong with alkali that if you only dip the most hopelessly soiled garment into them once or twice, and wring it out, it will be found as clean as if it had been through the ablest of washerwomen's hands. While we camped there our laundry work was easy. We tied the week's washing astern of our boat, and sailed a quarter of a mile, and the job was complete, all to the wringing out.

© DAVID MUENCH

Silver Fever

"By and by I was smitten with the silver fever. "Prospecting parties" were leaving for the mountains every day, and discovering and taking possession of rich, silver-bearing lodes and ledges of quartz. Plainly this was the road to fortune. And so on—day in and day out the talk pelted our ears and the excitement waxed hotter and hotter around us.

I would have been more or less than human if I had not gone mad like the rest. Cart-loads of solid silver bricks, as large as pigs of lead, were arriving from the mills every day, and such sights as that gave substance to the wild talk about me. I succumbed and grew as frenzied as the craziest.

Every few days news would come of the discovery of a brand new mining region; immediately the papers would teem with accounts of its richness, and away the surplus population would scamper to take possession. By the time I was fairly inoculated with the disease, "Esmeralda" had just had a run and "Humboldt" was beginning to shriek for attention. "Humboldt! Humboldt!" was the new cry, and straightway Humboldt, the newest of the new, the richest of the rich, the most marvelous of the marvelous discoveries in silver-land was occupying two columns of the public prints to "Esmeralda's"

COMSTOCK HISTORIC DISTRICT COMMISSION

Miners in Virginia City, Nevada, in the 1860s, before going underground. Comstock residents took pride in prohibiting child labor, so the boy was either the minimum age of fifteen or he was a visitor.

one. I was just on the point of starting to Esmeralda, but turned with the tide and got ready for Humboldt.

True knowledge of the nature of silver mining came fast enough. We went out "prospecting" with Mr. Ballou. We climbed the mountain sides, and clambered among sage-brush, rocks and snow till we were ready to drop with exhaustion, but found no silver— nor yet any gold. Day after day we did this. Now and then we came upon holes burrowed a few feet into the declivities and apparently abandoned; and now and then we found one or two listless men still burrowing. But there was no appearance of silver. These holes were the beginnings of tunnels, and the purpose was to drive them hundreds of feet into the mountain, and some day tap the hidden ledge where the silver was. Some day! It seemed far enough away, and very hopeless and dreary. Day after day we toiled, and climbed and searched, and we younger partners grew sicker and still sicker of the promiseless toil. At last we halted under a beetling rampart of rock which projected from the earth high upon the mountain. Mr. Ballou broke off some fragments with a hammer, and examined them long and attentively with a small eye-glass; threw them away and broke off more; said this rock was

"Peaceful Valley Saloon" (1900) by C.M. Russell
With silver fever, Mark Twain said, "I would have been more or less than human if I had not gone mad like the rest."

quartz, and quartz was the sort of rock that contained silver. Contained it! I had thought that at least it would be caked on the outside of it like a kind of veneering. He still broke off pieces and critically examined them, now and then wetting the piece with his tongue and applying the glass. At last he exclaimed:

"We've got it!"

Virginia City

"The 'city' of Virginia roosted royally midway up the steep side of Mount Davidson, seven thousand two hundred feet above the level of the sea, and in the clear Nevada atmosphere was visible from a distance of fifty miles! It claimed a population of fifteen thousand to eighteen thousand, and all day long half of this little army swarmed the streets like

LIBRARY OF CONGRESS

Virginia City was quickly cobbled together after the big silver strikes in 1859. The town was rebuilt several times following disastrous fires. This map is called "Virginia City, Nevada Territory, 1861," published by Grafton T. Brown.

bees and the other half swarmed among the drifts and tunnels of the "Comstock," hundreds of feet down in the earth directly under those same streets. Often we felt our chairs jar, and heard the faint boom of a blast down in the bowels of the earth under the office.

The mountain side was so steep that the entire town had a slant to it like a roof. Each street was a terrace, and from each to the next street below the descent was forty or fifty feet. The fronts of the houses were level with the street they faced, but their rear first floors were propped on lofty stilts; a man could stand at a rear first floor window of a C street house and look down the chimneys of the row of houses below him facing D street. It was a laborious climb, in that thin atmosphere, to ascend from D to A street, and you were panting and out of breath when you got there; but you could turn around and go down again like a house a-fire—so to speak.

From Virginia's airy situation one could look over a vast, far-reaching panorama of mountain ranges and deserts; and whether the day was bright or overcast, whether the sun was rising or setting, or flaming in the zenith, or whether night and the moon held sway, the spectacle was always impressive and beautiful. Over your head Mount Davidson lifted its gray dome, and before and below you a rugged canyon clove the battlemented hills, making a somber gateway through which a soft-tinted desert was glimpsed, with the silver thread of a river winding through it, bordered with trees which many miles of distance diminished to a delicate fringe: and still further away the snowy mountains rose up and stretched their long barrier to the filmy horizon—far enough beyond a lake that burned in the desert like a fallen sun, though that, itself, lay fifty miles removed. Look from your window where you would, there was fascination in the picture. At rare intervals—but very rare—there were clouds in our skies, and then the setting sun would gild and flush and glorify this mighty expanse of scenery with a bewildering pomp of color that held the eye like a spell and moved the spirit like music.

August Bouhaben ran a store in Virginia City. On March 31, 1892, as he ran to protect his partner who was being assaulted by a gunman, he was shot in the head. He died the next day. "Take that you damned foreigner," the gunman, Jerry Barry, yelled as he fled the scene firing his weapon wildly. Barry, who was a drunk and gambler, entered the store to secure monies being held in trust there. His pay as a miner was spent before he got home so the mining company put it in trust with the store so his family could eat and pay rent. Barry was given five dollars daily and when that was gone he armed himself to get more money. Barry was found by the sheriff hiding under his bed and six months later he was hanged. Bouhaben was buried in the Catholic Cemetery and his sister, Abel Laigneau, had a tombstone erected with the word "MURDERED" in caps put on the stone. She died about fifteen months later and is buried next to him. Photo © Marilyn Newton

The first twenty-six graves in the Virginia cemetery were occupied by murdered men. So everybody said, so everybody believed, and so they will always say and believe. The reason why there was so much slaughtering done, was, that in a new mining district the rough element predominates, and a person is not respected until he has "killed his man." That was the very expression used.

California poppies in Amador County. © *Larry Angier*

California

"We rumbled over the plains and valleys, climbed the Sierras to the clouds, and looked down upon summer-clad California. And I will remark here, in passing, that all scenery in California requires distance to give it its highest charm. The mountains are imposing in their sublimity and their majesty of form and altitude, from any point of view—but one must have distance to soften their ruggedness and enrich their tintings; a Californian forest is best at a little distance, for there is a sad poverty of variety in species, the trees being chiefly of one monotonous family—redwood, pine, spruce, fir—and so, at a near view there is a wearisome sameness of attitude in their rigid arms, stretched downward and outward in one continued and reiterated appeal to all men to "Sh!—don't say a word!—you might disturb somebody!""

San Francisco is built on sand hills, but they are prolific sand hills. They yield a generous vegetation. All the rare flowers which people in "the States" rear with such patient care in parlor flower-pots and green-houses,

flourish luxuriantly in the open air there all the year round. Calla lilies, all sorts of geraniums, passion flowers, moss roses—I do not know the names of a tenth part of them. I only know that while New Yorkers are burdened with banks and drifts of snow, Californians are burdened with banks and drifts of flowers, if they only keep their hands off and let them grow.

In Sacramento it is fiery summer always, and you can gather roses, and eat strawberries and ice-cream, and

Busy Market Street of the City of the Golden Gate, San Francisco, California, ca. 1901.

wear white linen clothes, and pant and perspire, at night or nine o'clock in the morning, and then take the cars, and

COURTESY WILLIAM J. CUMMINGS

Twain was duly impressed by the cornucopia of vegetation he found flourishing in California. He might not be surprised that the state supplies the United States with ninety-nine percent of its grapes and peaches and nearly that much of tomatoes and everything else on the national salad plate. A wine vineyard (above) in Sonoma County and a farmer's market (right) in Sacramento County.
Opposite: *A prospector pans for gold.*

© JOHN BARDWELL PHOTOS

at noon put on your furs and your skates, and go skimming over frozen Donner Lake, seven thousand feet above the valley, among snow banks fifteen feet deep, and in the shadow of grand mountain peaks that lift their frosty crags ten thousand feet above the level of the sea.

There is a transition for you! Where will you find another like it in the Western hemisphere? And some of us have swept around snow-walled curves of the Pacific Railroad in that vicinity, six thousand feet above the sea, and looked down as the birds do, upon the deathless Summer of the

Sacramento Valley, with its fruitful fields, its feathery foliage, its silver streams, all slumbering in the mellow haze of its enchanted atmosphere, and all infinitely softened and spiritualized by distance—a dreamy, exquisite glimpse of fairyland, made all the more charming and striking that it was caught through a forbidden gateway of ice and snow, and savage crags and precipices.

"At last we shouldered our pans and shovels and struck out over the hills to try new localities. We prospected around Angels Camp, in Calaveras county, during three weeks, but had no success. Then we wandered on foot among the mountains, sleeping under the trees at night, for the weather was mild, but still we remained as centless as the last rose of summer. That is a poor joke, but it is in pathetic harmony with the circumstances, since we were so poor ourselves. In accordance with the custom of the country, our door had always stood open and our board welcome to tramping miners—they drifted along nearly every day, dumped there paust shovels by the threshold and took "pot luck" with us—and now on our own tramp we never found cold hospitality.

Our wanderings were wide and in many directions; and now I could give the reader a vivid description of the Big Trees and the marvels of the Yo Semite—but what has this reader done to me that I should persecute him? I will deliver him into the hands of less conscientious tourists and take his blessing. Let me be charitable, though I fail in all virtues else.

NOTE: Within three months, Mark Twain was on his way to the Sandwich Islands—aka Hawaii, which became a state in 1959—to send back articles to the Sacramento Union newspaper.

The California Gold Rush began on January 24, 1848, when gold was found by James W. Marshall at Sutter's Mill in Coloma, California. The news of gold brought approximately 300,000 people to California from the rest of the United States and abroad.

The Celebrated Jumping Frog of Calaveras County

Mark Twain was in Angels Camp trying his hand at gold prospecting in Califorinia when he heard this tale told in a saloon. The prospecting was a bust but he hit gold when his version of the story was published.

"In compliance with the request of a friend of mine who wrote me from the East, I called on good-natured, garrulous old Simon Wheeler and inquired after my friend's friend, Leonidas W. Smiley, as requested to do, and I hereunto append the result. I have a lurking suspicion that *Leonidas W. Smiley* is a myth, that my friend never knew such a personage, and that he only conjectured that if I asked old Wheeler about him, it would remind him of his infamous *Jim* Smiley and he would go to work and bore me nearly to death with some infernal reminiscence of him as long and as tedious as it should be useless to me. If that was the design, it succeeded.

I found Simon Wheeler dozing comfortably by the bar-room stove of the dilapidated tavern in the decayed mining camp of Angels, and I noticed that he was fat and bald-headed, and had an expression of winning gentleness and simplicity upon his tranquil countenance. He roused up and gave me good-day. I told him that a friend of mine had commissioned me to make some inquiries about a cherished companion of his boyhood named Leonidas W. Smiley—*Rev. Leonidas W. Smiley,* a young minister of the Gospel, who he had heard was at one time a resident of Angels Camp. I added that if Mr. Wheeler could tell me anything about this Rev. Leonidas W. Smiley, I would feel under many obligations to him.

Simon Wheeler backed me into a corner and blockaded me there with his chair, and then sat down and reeled off the monotonous narrative which follows this paragraph. He never smiled, he never frowned, he never changed his voice from the gentle-flowing key to which he tuned his initial sentence, he never betrayed the slightest suspicion of enthusiasm, but all through the interminable narrative there ran a vein of impressive earnestness and sincerity which showed me plainly that, so far from his imagining that there was anything ridiculous or funny about his story, he regarded it as a really important matter and admired its two heroes as men of transcendent genius in *finesse.* (To me, the spectacle of a man drifting serenely along through such a queer yarn without ever smiling, was exquisitely absurd. As I said before, I asked him to tell me what he knew of Rev. Leonidas W. Smiley, and he replied as follows.) I let him go on in his own way and never interrupted him once....

"If it's your job to eat a frog, it's best to do it first thing in the morning. And if it's your job to eat two frogs, it's best to eat the biggest one first."

—Mark Twain

Leopard frog jumping into a pond. © Scott Linstead / Tom Stack & Associates

"Rev. Leonidas W., h'm, Reverend Le...well there was a feller here once by the name of *Jim* Smiley, in the winter of '49—or maybe it was the spring of '50—I don't recollect exactly, somehow, though what makes me think it was one or the other is because I remember the big flume wasn't finished when he first come to the camp; but any way, he was the curiousest man about always betting on anything that turned up you ever see, if he could get anybody to bet on the other side, and if he couldn't he'd change sides. Any way that suited the other man would suit *him*—any way just so's he got a bet, *he* was satisfied. But still he was lucky, uncommon lucky; he most always come out winner. He was always ready and laying for a chance; there couldn't be no solittry thing mentioned but that feller'd offer to bet on it and take any side you please, as I was just telling you. If there was a horserace, you'd find him flush, or you'd find him busted at the end of it; if there was a dog-fight, he'd bet on it; if there was a cat-fight, he'd bet on it; if there was a chicken-fight, he'd bet on it; why, if there was two birds setting on a fence, he would bet you which one would fly first; or if there was a camp-meeting, he would be there reg'lar to bet on Parson Walker, which he judged to be the best exhorter about here, and so he was too, and a good man. If he even seen a straddle-bug start to go anywhere, he would bet you how long it would take him to get to—to wherever he was going to, and if you took him up, he would foller that straddle-bug to Mexico but what he would find out where he was bound for and how long he was on the road. Lots of the boys here has seen that Smiley and can tell you about him. Why, it never made no difference to *him*—he'd bet on *any* thing—the dangdest feller. Parson Walker's wife laid very sick once for a

Joseph Kitchell of Angels Camp was winner of the 2005 Calaveras Frog Jump with his frog Roy W, named after Roy Weimer, who was the last Calaveras County resident to win the frog jump in 1954. © Larry Angier

good while, and it seemed as if they warn't going to save her; but one morning he come in and Smiley up and asked him how she was, and he said she was considerable better—thank the Lord for his inf'nite mercy—and coming on so smart that with the blessing of Prov'dence, she'd get well yet;

and Smiley, before he thought, says, 'Well, I'll risk two-and-a-half that she don't—anyway.'

"Thish-yer Smiley had a mare—the boys called her the fifteen-minute nag but that was only in fun, you know, because of course she was faster than that—and he used to win money on that horse, for all she was so slow and always had the asthma, or the distemper, or the consumption, or something of that kind. They used to give her two or three hundred yards' start and then pass her under way, but always at the fag end of the race she'd get excited and desperate like, and come cavorting and straddling up and scattering her legs around limber, sometimes in the air and sometimes out to one side amongst the fences, and kicking up m-o-r-e dust and raising m-o-r-e racket with her coughing and sneezing and blowing her nose—and *always* fetch up at the stand just about a neck ahead, as near as you could cipher it down.

"And he had a little small bull-pup, that to look at him you'd think he warn't worth a cent, but to set around and look ornery and lay for a chance to steal something. But as soon as money was up on him he was a different dog; his under-jaw'd begin to stick out like the fo'castle of a steamboat, and his teeth would uncover and shine like the furnaces. And a dog might tackle him, and bully-rag him, and bite him and throw him over his shoulder two or three times, and Andrew Jackson—which was the name of the pup—

Andrew Jackson would never let on but what *he* was satisfied and hadn't expected nothing else—and the bets being doubled and doubled on the other side all the time, till the money was all up; and then all of a sudden he would grab that other dog jest by the j'int of his hind leg and freeze to it—not chaw, you understand, but only jest grip and hang on till they throwed up the sponge, if it was a year. Smiley always come out winner on that pup till he harnessed a dog once that didn't have no hind legs, because they'd been sawed off in a circular saw, and when the thing had gone along far enough and the money was all up and he come to make a snatch for his pet holt, he see in a minute how he'd been imposed on and how the other dog had him in the door, so to speak, and he 'peered surprised, and then he looked rather discouraged-like and didn't try no more to win the fight, and so he got shucked out bad. He give Smiley a look, as much as to say his heart was broke, and it was *his* fault for putting up a dog that hadn't no hind legs for him to take holt of, which was his main dependence in a fight, and then he limped off a piece and laid down and died. It was a good pup, was that Andrew Jackson, and would have made a name for hisself if he'd lived, for the stuff was in him, and he had genius—I know it, because he hadn't had no opportunities to speak of, and it don't stand to reason that a dog could make such a fight as he could under

them circumstances if he hadn't no talent. It always makes me feel sorry when I think of that last fight of his'n and the way it turned out.

"Well, thish-yer Smiley had rat-tarriers, and chicken cocks, and tom-

JUMPING FROG © SCOTT LINSTEAD/TOM STACK & ASSOCIATES

cats, and all of them kind of things till you couldn't rest, and you couldn't fetch nothing for him to bet on but he'd match you. He ketched a frog one day and took him home, and said he cal'k-lated to educate him; and so he never done nothing for three months but set in his back yard and learn that frog to jump. And you bet you he *did* learn him, too. He'd give him a little punch behind, and the next minute you'd see that frog whirling in the air like a doughnut—see him turn one summer-set, or maybe a couple if he got a good start, and come down flat-footed and all right, like a cat. He got him up so in the matter of ketching flies, and kep' him in practice so constant, that he'd nail a fly every time as fur as he could see him. Smiley said all a frog wanted was education, and he could do most anything—and I believe him. Why, I've seen him set Dan'l Webster down here on this floor—Dan'l Webster was the name of the frog—and sing out, 'Flies, Dan'l, flies!' and quicker'n you could wink he'd spring straight up and snake a fly off'n the counter there, and flop down on the floor ag'in as solid as a gob of mud, and fall to scratching the side of his head with his hind foot as indifferent as if he hadn't no idea he'd been doin' any more'n any frog might do. You never see a frog so modest and straightforward as he was, for all he was so gifted. And when it come to fair and square jumping on a dead level, he could get over more ground at one straddle than any animal of his breed you ever see. Jumping on a dead level was his strong suit, you understand; and when it come to that, Smiley would ante up money on him as long as he had a red. Smiley was monstrous proud of his frog, and well he might be for fellers that had traveled and been everywheres all said he laid over any frog that ever they see.

"Well, Smiley kept the beast in a little lattice box, and he used to fetch him down-town sometimes and lay for a bet. One day a feller—a stranger in the camp, he was—come acrost him with his box and says:

"'What might it be that you've got in the box?'

"And Smiley says, sorter indifferent-like, 'It might be a parrot, or it might be a canary, maybe, but it ain't—it's only just a frog.'

"And the feller took it, and looked at it careful, and turned it round this way and that, and says, 'H'm—so 'tis. Well, what's he good for?'

"'Well,' Smiley says, easy and careless, 'he's good enough for one thing, I should judge—he can outjump any frog in Calaveras County.'

"The feller took the box again and took another long, particular look, and give it back to Smiley and says, very deliberate, 'Well,' he says, 'I don't see no p'ints about that frog that's any better'n any other frog.'

"'Maybe you don't,' Smiley says. 'Maybe you understand frogs and maybe you don't understand 'em; maybe you've had experience and maybe you ain't only a amature, as it were. Anyways, I've got my opinion, and I'll risk forty dollars that he can outjump any frog in Calaveras County.'

"And the feller studied a minute and then says, kinder sad-like, 'Well, I'm only a stranger here and I ain't got no frog, but if I had a frog, I'd bet you.'

"And then Smiley says, 'That's all right—that's all right—if you'll hold my box a minute, I'll go and get you a frog.' And so the feller took the box and put up his forty dollars along with Smiley's, and set down to wait.

"So he set there a good while thinking and thinking to hisself, and then he got the frog out and prized his mouth open and took a teaspoon and filled him full of quail-shot—filled him pretty near up to his chin—and set him on the floor. Smiley he went to the swamp and slopped around in the mud for a long time, and finally he ketched